A SHORT HISTORY OF SPAGHETTI WITH TOMATO SAUCE

Massimo Montanari

A SHORT HISTORY
OF SPAGHETTI
WITH TOMATO SAUCE

*Translated from the Italian
by Gregory Conti*

Europa
editions

Europa Editions
8 Blackstock Mews
London N4 2BT
www.europaeditions.co.uk

Translation by Gregory Conti
Original title: *Il mito delle origini. Breve storia degli spaghetti al pomodoro*
Translation copyright © 2021 by Europa Editions

A catalogue record for this title is available from the British Library
ISBN 978-1-78770-328-5

Montanari, Massimo
A Short History of Spaghetti with Tomato Sauce

Book design and cover illustration by Emanuele Ragnisco
www.mekkanografici.com

Inside illustrations by Ginevra Rapisardi

Prepress by Grafica Punto Print – Rome

Printed and bound in Great Britain by Clays Ltd, Elcograf S.p.A.

CONTENTS

Birth, what does that mean?
Dear Doctor, what matters is growth,
And, modestly, that little lady there has had some growth . . .
Whoa!
Totò in Paris, 1958

A SHORT HISTORY OF SPAGHETTI WITH TOMATO SAUCE

WORDS: HANDLE WITH CARE

The "Idol of Origins." That's what Marc Bloch, the greatest European historian of the XX century, called it.[1] Searching the past for what paved the way for the present, according to Bloch, is an obsession typical of those who concern themselves with history. It also dominates the collective imagination. Nothing wrong with that, on the face of it. It all depends on what you mean by origins. Simply the "beginnings"? In that case, the concept is fairly clear. Or does it also mean "causes"? In that case, what we're looking at is a historical determinism that is both naïve and unsustainable, as well as contradicted by experience. Given a point of departure X, there is no single destination Y but rather a multiplicity of possible directions, defined by circumstances, the interaction of various forces, chance, and the unforeseeable.

The problem is that these two interpretations are often combined in a logical misstep. "In popular usage, an origin is a beginning which explains. Worse still, a beginning which is a complete explanation." That's where the ambiguity lies, the danger. Confusing lineage with explanation. Because an acorn is not an oak tree.

Bloch's metaphor is brilliant. "Great oaks from little acorns grow. But only if they meet favorable conditions of soil and climate, conditions which are entirely beyond the scope of embryology." And this is what really interests the historian, the analysis of the environmental conditions, the economic, social, and cultural humus that allow the acorn to become an oak tree. From that perspective, are the origins really all that important?

Actually, origins don't explain anything, because a seed is necessary to give life to a plant, but not sufficient to generate a root, and, from it, a plant. That's what "origins" really are, not a cause but simply a seed that *can* turn into a plant, providing it encounters a favorable environment. The key word here is *encounter*. The more numerous and more interesting the encounters, the richer the result, the stronger and more robust the plant. In this way, it will have constructed its own identity, which, like all products of history, is *alive* and changeable. Alive *because* it is changeable—"movement is the cause of all life" is the celebrated phrase of Leonardo Da Vinci. With regard to the roots that have made this identity possible, throwing oneself into the search for them is an experience that can turn out to be more adventurous than expected, leading us to visit places, societies, and cultures that are not necessarily our own.

Roots and *identity* are perilous words, to be handled with care. Too often, they are misunderstood and confused, when it is important to distinguish them. Roots inhabit the past. On the time line, if we want to recount the birth, growth, and development of anything, they are at the beginning, and they expand in space to take nourishment from every reachable source (the botanical metaphor, if it is to be useful, must be squeezed to its full potential). At the other end of the time line are identities, which, instead, inhabit the present—a mobile present, always intent on projecting itself into the future all the while becoming itself the past. At any point on the chronological line, identities are a destination: characterized by well-defined mental and material spaces, but always unstable and changeable, as is proper to everything that lives.

Losing sight of the *vitality* of identities means denying oneself a truly *historical* outlook on them and the roots from which they spring, or their "origins." It means thinking of them as *immutable* with respect to the future, devoting oneself not to keeping them alive—with the opportune adaptations—but to freezing them, codifying them, confining them to museums. It means thinking of them as *immutable* with respect to the past—a past that thus becomes pure legend and a colossal mystification. It is the idol of origins that crops up again, against all evidence, against all logic. And this justifies the radical choices of those who do not limit themselves to recommending caution in the use of these concepts and terminology but oppose them to the point of eliminating them from the vocabulary and from the collective imagination. *Against Roots* is the title of a book by Maurizio Bettini,[2] *Against Identity* is a book by Francesco Remotti,[3] to cite just two exemplary cases. This little essay could have been called *Against Origins*. But the historian holds on to the illusion that the simple recounting of the facts can help to shed light on the meaning of words and things. Especially when the "things" are aspects of the life that we confront on a daily basis. For example, food, food products, and cooking recipes.

Is it possible to sit down to a plate of spaghetti with tomato sauce and reflect on the meaning of roots, identities, and origins? That is what I have tried to do in these pages.

RECIPES AND PRODUCTS,
OR RATHER, TIME AND SPACE

When we eat, and when we talk about food, misunderstandings and mystifications are part of the agenda, and they have a strong emotional impact. Indeed, everything that regards food and the dining table evokes profound values and sensations connected to personal identity. As always, material reality (our ways of living) and mental reality (our ways of thinking) interact and, in this case as in others—perhaps more than in others—our imagination is conditioned by prejudices, clichés, myths, fantasies, and *idols*. The idol of origins is the most powerful and it forces itself on the individual and collective consciousness, in terms of both time and space.

Time is the dimension of *recipes*, whose origins we often try to find by searching for some specific episode, the exact moment when someone had the idea to make it for the very first time. An age-old obsession. *Catalogue of the inventors of things that we eat and drink* is the semi-serious title of a curious work by the Milanese humanist Ortensio Lando, published in 1548. Combing through ancient literature and adding a lot from his own imagination, he delights in recounting who was the first to "eat rosemary and elderberry pancakes," or to "fry bread in butter," or to "eat a soup of barley and ground oats."[4]

In this case, the myth of the origins rises to the level of

method—albeit in a humorous way—but we all know stories and anecdotes that ascribe this or that recipe to improbable historical figures: the chef, the lord, the monk are the most frequent suspects, but there is no lack of shepherds and farmers in an explosive mix of lucky coincidences, and inventions compelled by hunger, chance, and happenstance. The important thing is to establish an origin, which calms and reassures. No matter that, in this way, *fiction* takes the place of history. Even if nobody really believes it, the narrative is so attractive that it satisfies in any case. It satisfies the desire to know, the urgency of recognizing a certain origin one can appeal to, because there, at the origin, lies the secret of history; because, to return to Bloch, origins are thought to be not a simple beginning but rather a "beginning which explains." About all the rest (which economic and social dynamics produced the recipe and which, vice versa, it set in motion; how and why, and in which kind of culture it carved out a role for itself; what place it came to occupy in the culinary system) we can happily forget about. While we were pretending to heed the call of history, we were actually ignoring history altogether.

Space is the dimension of food *products*. Contemporary rhetoric—especially, but not exclusively, in the language of marketing and advertising—has taught us to call it *territory*, insisting on that word and concept to the point of obsession. It is the territory that confers on products their identifying mark, their "origin"—understood exactly in the way it was deplored by Bloch. Not simply the place in which a product is born, but that which magically attributes to it an identity. Here, too, origins become a "beginning which explains."

Sure, we all know that the territory by itself is not

enough to "explain" a product, its characteristics and qualities. The hand of humanity, which, by interacting with the environment and exploiting natural resources, plays a major role in *inventing* that product, is at least as important. This is accounted for by the French term *terroir*, which combines the geography of place with human skills. This is also taken into account by the regulations of agricultural consortiums, which establish precise norms—techniques, procedures, methods—for granting to a certain product the right to boast a certain geographical origin, marking it as "typical" of a certain place.

This operation is not devoid of ambiguity. On the one hand, it allows for the safeguarding and protection of a common good, by subjecting it to rigorous production and marketing controls. On the other hand, it expropriates that good, by turning it over to private management, which is what consortiums are, even though they are publicly authorized. But what I want to emphasize here is the *idolatrous* prospect that the notion of "origin" takes on in all of this. The word acquires the value of, so to speak, an almost *ontological* guarantee of the nature and quality of the product. "Origin" becomes a value in and of itself.

This is not to say that emphasis on the territory is exclusive to modern times or the global market—since identifying something, or someone, with a name of territorial origin makes sense only after, and as far as, that something or that someone leaves that territory to circulate elsewhere. This has always been true. Ancient texts (those written by Latin agronomists, for example) are rife with local attributions referring to products, and the gastronomic literature of the Middle Ages and the Renaissance is overflowing with geographical origin names. The intention here—rather than some normative anxiety—is always to recognize, compare, and promote. Even the Renaissance humanist Bartolomeo Platina, when speaking of Padua hens or Viterbo carrots, or any number of local specialties,[5] assigns to a place a value of quality and guarantee. And, in his case, there are no commercial consortia putting on the pressure. Therefore, the territory, geography, place appear to be a constant of the collective imagination related to the pleasure of food.

Nor am I trying to say that origins are irrelevant; the evidence belies that. But I wish to emphasize how this attention to origins, in itself fully justified, may take on disturbing significance, when it is combined with mental attitudes that are sometimes tinged with intolerance and fanaticism. That happens when the legitimate idea "my cooking is good" turns into "my cooking is good because its (and my) origin is good." Better than yours, that is. That's how origins are put into conflict with one another, without realizing that history—there it is again, history, time that disturbs the peace of place—demonstrates the contrary, namely, that mixing people and things and drawing on different "origins" often produces excellent and in any case dynamic results, and life goes on and everything becomes more interesting.

In reality, products (the exemplary case of the appeal to "origins") never work by themselves. Cooking mixes them and puts them into play, making them interact. Basil is exquisite, but nobody eats basil by itself. Chili peppers are exquisite, but nobody eats just chili peppers. Pasta is exquisite, but nobody eats pasta without sauce. To be sure, cooking starts with ingredients but, above all, it relies on recipes. "Recipes" from the Latin *recipio*: I take (from here, from there, what I need) and I compose. Even the most autochthonous recipes, the ones based on "local" products, are never so completely local as to exclude contributions from diverse origins.

Reflecting on a Plate of Pasta

It is beyond dispute that pasta is a culinary symbol of Italian identity, the perfect image of a culture (not only gastronomical) which paradoxically finds its distinctive and unifying element in the multiplicity of its local variations.[6] Hundreds of shapes and thousands of recipes, made from different products and with different procedures, are tied to individual cities and rural areas, which recognize in those preparations different histories, traditions, and tastes, disseminating throughout the country a food culture without equal in terms of variety and unpredictability. Each shape, each preparation has its own history, recounts particular experiences and tastes, closely or not-so-closely tied to local production or market supply. This incredible variety of shapes and flavors, which the food industry tends to shrink—not being able to represent them all—but has no interest in eliminating, all comes down to one word and once substance, *pasta*, which has long been the icon of Italian cooking.

Icons within the icon, some recipes and some shapes stand out from the others, establishing themselves as primary symbols of the national cuisine. Spaghetti with tomato sauce, especially if topped with grated parmigiano cheese, is the symbol of national identity par excellence. At least that is how it is perceived from outside—and we know that identities, even before becoming the "internal" glue of a community, are nourished by external perspectives, which necessarily simplify and synthesize, as, when taking a photograph, you go from zoom to wide angle, obscuring the details in favor of the overall picture. "In the eyes of the uninformed foreigner," Odile Redon and Bruno Laurioux have written, the premier Italian dish "is none other than a plate of spaghetti with tomato sauce and grated parmigiano."[7]

Let's ruminate a bit then over this dish. Inquiring into its *origins* is certainly legitimate. Curiosity is the engine of all discoveries. But it is equally licit to say, right from the start and heeding the warning of Marc Bloch, that we are not so interested in finding out (if it were at all possible) who was the first to have the idea of making it, or who was the first to taste it. Rather, we are interested in investigating the "environmental conditions"—the places, the itineraries—that made it possible to "raise" the idea, taking it all the way to the good fortune of becoming, *today*, the identifying mark of a cuisine and a culture.

The historian must, therefore, establish relationships and chronologies, identify causes and effects, ascertain, somewhere between the opposing ideas of destiny and chance, that much more effective idea of the circumstances and the *opportunity*—the *Kairos* of the Greeks—that is, the will and the capability of recognizing an opportunity and profiting from it to make something useful. In order to do this, we will have to move back and forth. *Back*, to find the "roots" that make possible the existence of this dish (roots in the plural, since a recipe is a complex creation, which requires interaction between different seeds, acorns of various provenance). *Forth*, in the search for the environmental conditions that at a certain point ensure its success, the grafting of this dish onto Italian tradition.

I will thus propose a sort of *historical deconstruction* of the dish, in the hunt for its constitutive elements—the ingredients of which it is composed, and the techniques with which they are prepared, assembled, and transformed. But not only. Beyond the basic products and the procedures through which they take shape, our attention will also be focused on the ways this dish is used, since every cuisine has the configuration of a *system*, within which every element occupies a precise place—like a word in a sentence—and takes on a specific meaning. The logic and the "grammar" of the system, therefore, will be equally important in evaluating the role (as well as the characteristics) of our plate of spaghetti.

But first of all, what elements should we choose? After all, the variety characteristic of Italian cuisine—never, fortunately, codified or reduced to homogenous and conforming models—is found in each single recipe, susceptible to infinite variation in local, social, and generational customs. There are so many versions of this plate of spaghetti with tomato sauce that we have decided to analyze!

So let's choose a minimum common denominator, a standard that will satisfy, if not everybody, most people. The basic elements will be, obviously, spaghetti and tomato sauce. And the same goes for grated parmigiano—a less obvious choice, but equally important in the collective imagination (Redon and Laurioux have already demonstrated this to us, and historical analysis confirms it). Let's add olive oil, calling it simply that, leaving out the "extra" and the "virgin," terms that only today have acquired a precise meaning in merchandising and marketing. Let's add garlic and/or onion (choose one or the other or both together, it's just a question of taste). We won't deny ourselves a basil leaf, by now a commonplace of Italian identity. Salt. We could stop here, but a pinch of chili pepper is suggested in the majority of recipes.

MARCO POLO AND SPAGHETTI:
THE BIRTH OF A FAKE NEWS ITEM

In 1989, the review *Médiévales* published an investigative report devoted to the comparative history of pasta in various parts of the world. The title of the report was *Against Marco Polo*[8] and the objective was to dismantle the legend that Marco Polo, on his return from China at the end of the XIII century, introduced pasta to Italy—a notion that continues unabashed to spark the imagination of lots of pasta lovers. It is false. There is no mention of it in any of the manuscripts of Polo's *The Million*, which instead talks about sago flour (the starch extracted from a particular species of palm) that the inhabitants of Sumatra use to make "lasagna and other types of pasta," products that reminded Marco Polo of analogous preparations well known to him, long consumed in Italy.

The misunderstanding is born two centuries later, when Giovanni Battista Ramusio, then publishing the travel memoirs of the Venetian merchant, misunderstands and manipulates the text. Ramusio transfers information about pasta made from sago (of which Marco Polo, fascinated by it, decides to bring a sample back to Venice) to pasta in general, making readers believe that Marco had discovered the secret of pasta in China.[9]

This is in 1559, and since then the fable has kept on proliferating, reinforced by some wild inventions, including an especially remarkable one by an American journalist. In 1929, writing in the *Macaroni Journal*, the official organ of the pasta industry association, he attributes the discovery to one of Marco Polo's sailors, a Venetian named Spaghetti(!). Having gotten off the boat in search of water, this Spaghetti happens upon a farm woman who is stirring a bowl of semi-liquid batter, which then, in the hot dry climate of Cathay, solidifies. The sailor has an intuition: a dry food, able to last, could be useful on long sea voyages. He gets the woman to give him a bit of that batter—some strings of it that have stuck to the rim of the bowl—and rushes back to the ship in excitement. He kneads and pulls the pasta into long strips, thus creating spaghetti, which takes its name from its inventor. Now all he has to do is cook it, and he decides to boil it in salt water from the sea. On the ship's return to Italy, the dish is a triumph.[10]

Let's move on to more serious things, trying to summarize the terms of a question that is actually quite complicated—the kind of thing that is not popular among lovers of anecdotes and imaginary stories, which are so enjoyable and reassuring. The history of pasta, in fact, remains obscure in some of its important points, even though it has been carefully studied by scholars, who have managed to clarify its essentials.

First of all, we need to reiterate China's complete lack of involvement in the "Western" history of pasta. Not because China didn't (and doesn't still) have a starring role in the history of pasta. The Chinese tradition has developed extraordinary skills and techniques in this sector, well-documented going back to the most ancient times. However, that tradition has followed its own routes, different and autonomous with respect to the development of the culture of pasta in the Western world, especially in Italy.

Scholars—especially Françoise Sabban[11]—have amply illustrated the substantial differences between these two histories, which have never really met. In China, the culture of pasta has always been confined to the use of common or soft wheat and to the domestic preparation of the product, for immediate family use. In Italy, on the other hand, along with an analogous tradition of fresh pasta, there was a precocious development—starting, as we shall see, in the Middle Ages—of an artisanal-industrial production of pasta, based on the use of durum wheat and the fabrication of dried pasta with a long shelf life.

In any case, the Chinese pasta tradition has had no relationship with Italy. The Italian pasta tradition has been influenced by other histories, other "roots," which evoke other cultures and other regions of the world. The search for "origins," in this case, takes us to the Fertile Crescent, the Middle Eastern regions to the east of the Mediterranean, where, ten to twelve thousand years ago, the agricultural revolution began, and with it, the culture of wheat and its derivatives—first among them, bread, which became the symbol of that revolution.

BREAD AND PASTA:
FROM THE MIDDLE EAST TO EUROPE

P asta was born as a variation on this unleavened (but sometimes leavened) bread, occasionally dried to enhance conservation. The bread that certain ancient texts call "Asian bread," because of its origin, perhaps Egyptian, perhaps Mesopotamian, perhaps both.[12] This thin dough, flattened with a rolling pin or worked by hand into elongated or other shapes, was called by Sasanian era Persians (III-VII centuries) *lakhsha*. Another term, *rishta*, indicated more precisely a type of pasta cut in strips or strings (like tagliatelle or spaghetti) before being dried.[13] The term seems quite ancient; the Iranian language may have derived it from a *risnatu*, of which there has remained a trace in a cuneiform tablet from almost 4000 years ago. The tablet conserves recipes from Akkadian and Sumerian tradition—the oldest agricultural societies in the world.[14]

Having traveled from the Middle East to Europe, the practice of rolling dough also appears in the Greek and Romano-Hellenistic world. *Làganon* in Greek and *lagana* in Latin are the terms used to indicate it, but with an ambiguous meaning, since they sometimes appear to refer to an item similar to Italian lasagna (which gets its name from these terms) and other times to crêpes, biscuits, or similar forms[15]—the great family of unleavened breads.[16]

The gesture of "pulling" dough alludes to another Latin term, *tracta*, from *trahere*, which means "to pull," attested in the only complete Roman cookbook that has come down to us, attributed to Apicius.[17]

The Greco-Roman gastronomic culture, however, does not recognize pasta as a *genus* of food. The Greeks and Romans limit themselves to making it, using it (fresh or dried) as an ingredient for this or that recipe—to wrap a filling, thicken a broth, etc.—but they do not think of it and do not describe it as a "family" of dishes related to each other by common types of fabrication, preparation, and use. Something that, today, we take for granted.

In the Greco-Roman world, the difficulty of thinking of pasta as a *genus* was tied to the anomalous nature of the product compared to then current gastronomic practices, models, and conceptions. Sabban and Serventi[18] have dubbed pasta "unthinkable," in ancient Mediterranean cultures. They note that, in those cultures, the large variety of ways of using grains can be reduced to two basic types: the bread and savory cake model, more or less leavened doughs that were cooked in the dry heat of the oven; and the polenta and grain soup model (depending on whether the grains were ground into flour or used whole) that were cooked in the humid heat of water or broth.

The pasta that is familiar to us—a batter of flour or semolina that is cooked in water—did not enter into this binary scheme, and was therefore an ambiguous preparation, "unthinkable," that is, to the extent it mixed and contaminated the two recognized models. Also for this reason, the most normal way of preparing Roman *lagana*—when the word referred to something like our lasagna—was by frying or baking without first boiling the noodles in water. And in some cases, the *lagana* was leavened like bread. Even in the Middle Ages, an Italian cookbook called for *fermented dough* for making lasagna.[19]

Actually, there is already talk of pasta cooked in liquid in imperial Rome,[20] but these are sporadic, marginal references. More meaningful, because it reveals the existence of a coherent discussion on the merits, is the testimony of certain Hebrew texts from the III-IV centuries, from which we learn that this custom, although practiced in the domestic environment, was nonetheless perceived as anomalous. The *Talmud of Jerusalem* excludes boiled pasta from the religious context, omitting it from the normal offering of food products for the clergy.[21] Such disputes are sufficient in any case to prove the existence, already in those centuries, in the eastern part of the Roman Empire, of a new type of dough (and of a new way of cooking it) for which the *Talmud* uses a special name, *itrium*, destined to have great success in succeeding centuries.

NEW NAMES FOR A NEW PRODUCT

The idea of drying pasta was in some sense inherent to the type of product: any dough, once "pulled," can be dried and conserved for some time. Apicius's *tracta*[22] was dry, as had also been, probably, the Mesopotamian *risnatu* of two thousand years earlier. The practice of drying was used most frequently on long-shaped pasta, like the Persian *rishta*, which lent itself particularly well to drying, especially when the product was made from durum wheat. The coming together of these factors (the type of wheat, the shape of the pasta, the custom of drying it) gradually came to constitute a new chapter in the history of pasta. The principal interpreters of this new phase were the Arabs, after conquering Persia at the beginning of the VII century, incorporating it into the Arab world, and assimilating its culture and traditions.

It is possible that the procedures for preparing dried pasta were introduced to the western Mediterranean by Jewish merchants. Pietro Ispano, writing in the Middle Ages, referred to dried pasta as "food of the Jews" (*cibus iudeorum*).[23] But it was the Arabs who spread the custom throughout the regions that they occupied and governed: North Africa, Sicily, and Andalusia. Thanks to their mediation, the new practice was superimposed on the Greek and Roman tradition of fresh pasta—itself, perhaps, the descendant of more ancient Middle Eastern models.

New names accompanied the appearance of the new product. Arab treatises on cooking and dietetics launch the term *itriyya*, analogue of the Hebrew *itrium* and very similar to the Greek *tria* (attested as far back as the VI century BCE), from which it may have derived. But in Greek, *tria* referred to various preparations, such as spiced breads, biscuits, or crêpes.[24] This is one reason why the Greek derivation of the term remains uncertain. Instead, according to some scholars, it is a term characteristic of Semitic languages—such as Arabic, Hebrew, Syriac, and Aramaic—albeit related in some way to Greek.[25] In any case, the Arab influence was decisive in transmitting this word to the West, where it entered into Medieval Latin in its new meaning of "long-form dried pasta." In the eastern part of the Islamic empire, this meaning continued to be attached to the word *rishta*, while *itriyya* took on a broader meaning, indicating pasta in general.[26]

Another new term, which made its appearance in the Middle Ages, is *fidawsh*, whose origin is almost certainly Arabic.[27] Unknown in the East, this term spread throughout the Western regions of the Islamic world to indicate pasta in general or, sometimes, more specifically, short pasta or pasta broken into pieces to thicken broth. Over the course of the centuries, the term would make its way into the principal neo-Latin languages. Italian, for example, would use the term *fedelini*.

THE SICILIAN MELTING POT AND THE BIRTH
OF THE PASTA INDUSTRY

At this point, our attention turns to Sicily, occupied in the IX century by the Arabs and continuously under Islamic domination for more than two hundred years, until the Norman conquest of the XI century. During this period, Sicily was deeply penetrated by Arab culture, which remained alive on the island even during the Norman occupation. It can be no coincidence, therefore, that precisely here, in the middle of the XII century, an extraordinary document attests the existence of a dried pasta industry; the first in history. An industry, moreover, which controls all phases of the productive cycle, from the harvesting and milling of the wheat to the fabrication and marketing of the pasta.

The account comes down to us from al-Idrisi, a North African nobleman who became an advisor to the Norman King Roger II—the cultural and political context of the time was extremely open-minded and featured collaboration among Christians, Jews, and Muslims. A geographer and traveler, al-Idrisi wrote (in Arabic) a *Book of Pleasant Journeys into Faraway Lands* also known as the *Tabula Rogeriana*, in which he describes cities and territories all around the Mediterranean. When he comes to write about Trabia—a locality in the vicinity of Palermo—he notes the presence of "perennial waters that move several mills" and of vast farms "where a lot of pasta [*itriyya*] is made for export to Calabria [referring to all of southern Italy] and to other Islamic and Christian countries"; and that "many shiploads of it are exported."[28]

This is the only passage of the book that talks about *itriyya*, or long-form dried pasta. The Sicilian establishments described by al-Idrisi must have been of remarkable importance, certainly on the cutting edge, and it comes as no surprise that Sicily returns frequently, in the literature of subsequent centuries, as a center of the culture of pasta, not only in terms of the export market but also with regard to local consumption. Until the 1500s, Sicilians would be identified with the epithet "macaroni eaters," which only later would come to be attributed to Neapolitans.[29]

The documented Sicilian activity from the XII century opens the way to the development of the pasta industry in Italy, in coastal areas, between ports and markets. Thanks to its capacity for conservation, dried pasta develops a manufacturing and commercial vocation.[30] Sicily's first competitor is the other great Mediterranean island, Sardinia, a pasta exporter ever since the XIII century, as demonstrated by the customs records in Cagliari.[31] Other pasta factories are established in Italian maritime cities such as Genoa, Pisa, and perhaps Amalfi. Genoa develops a flourishing import-export trade, bringing in pasta from Sicily or Sardinia and shipping it north by land or sea. For centuries, *pasta from Genoa* will be an obligatory reference point of Italian gastronomy, not necessarily tied to local production. Venice, too, imported (from Puglia) and exported pasta. Over time, Naples will also take on an important role and will then become dominant in the centuries to follow—we shall see further on how and why.

Looking beyond developments in individual cities or

regions, what happens over the course of several centuries—a decisive fact in the history of Italian cuisine—is the progressive spread of a nutritional practice and a productive activity that gradually grow in importance and move from a marginal to a central position. The fact that this change had its start in Sicily does not appear to be coincidental but tied, instead, to the convergence of certain "environmental conditions" that—as Block would say—allowed the seed to grow and put down roots.

One primary condition, the oldest, was the Hellenic cultural subsoil, thoroughly absorbed by Sicily in the centuries in which it was part of *Magna Graecia*—Greater Greece. Once it came under Roman domination, the island was assigned the role of the breadbasket of the empire, interpreting in an exemplary fashion the agricultural and dietary tradition of the Mediterranean. Sicily maintained very strong relations with the Roman and Hellenistic world into the early Middle Ages when it was under Byzantine domination. This accounts for its interception of, first, the Greek and then the Roman culture of *lagana* and fresh pasta. Between the IX and XI centuries, the Arab influence grafted onto this earlier Greco-Roman tradition, redesigning Sicilian food culture under the hallmark of dried pasta. This manner of preparing pasta may have already been introduced to the island by its Jewish communities, whose presence is documented as early as the first centuries of the Middle Ages.[32] Nevertheless, the central role that the Islamic world would later take on in the control of trade routes[33] must have been a determining factor in the promotion of dried pasta in a region like Sicily, which was obviously a strategic point in the maritime trade in the western Mediterranean.

To these conditions, shaped by history, we should add the "geographic" preconditions of the island's soil and climate, well-suited to the cultivation of wheat and particularly of durum wheat, the best raw material for dried pasta. Finally—getting back to history—we have to factor in the central role of the city in the social and civic organization of the Greek, Roman, and Hellenistic worlds; a condition that favored the development of food cultures typically tied to the marketplace and urban consumption, like that—obviously—of dried pasta.

But these conditions were only opportunities. Taking advantage of them, making them fruitful, turning them into the *core business* of a new gastronomic culture, was not at all an obvious conclusion. For one thing, the medieval dietary imagination nurtured a certain distrust of conserved foods, confining them, as a general rule, within the limits of "poor" foods, not exactly appropriate to be featured on the dinner tables of the elite.[34] How did it happen, then, that in the span of just a few centuries, spaghetti became an identity symbol of Italian cuisine?

WHEN SPAGHETTI WERE CALLED MACARONI

I n the earliest Italian cookbooks, which date back to the 1300 and 1400s, not much space was devoted to "industrial" dried pasta. *Tria* appears only rarely, just one recipe in the XIV century, two in the XV.[35] Long-form dried pasta seems to be referred to as *ancia alexandrina* in the XIV century *Liber de coquina* (The Book of Cookery), compiled by the Angevin royal court of Naples. Some have claimed that this volume dates back to a lost recipe collection from the preceding century, compiled at the Swabian court in Palermo during the reign of Frederick II.[36] This dish is made from "Apulian" wheat (*semola apula)* and the term *ancia* has been translated in Italian as "*tubo, cannello, vermicello*" (literally, tube, blow pipe, little worm).[37]

More frequent are recipes that use fresh dough to make little gastronomic masterpieces. Various forms are invented by way of the "miniaturization" of lasagna, a pioneering breakthrough of medieval cooking.[38] In the meantime, further developments are made in the culture of filled pasta—perhaps of Turco-Mongolian origin, and it, too, brought to the West by way of Arab mediation.[39] Filled pasta combines the ancient tradition of *lagana*, cut into smaller pieces, with the tradition, equally ancient but developed especially in Medieval times, of filled *torte* (savory pastries), from which were derived *tortelli* and *tortellini.*[40] Italy witnessed a veritable boom in filled pasta during the Middle Ages and the Renaissance.

In the recipe books, the description of the preparation procedures becomes increasingly precise. Maestro Martino, the most talented chef of XV century Italy, active in the papal court in the second half of the century, explains in detail how to make "Sicilian macaroni," *pastoncelli* (pasta sticks) obtained from a ball of dough, about a palm's length and as thin as a straw, *pertusati* (perforated) with a wire "thin as a *spagho*" (string).[41] Macaroni "*romaneschi*," on the other hand, are extracted from a sheet of dough in a way similar to *tagliatelle* or *fettucine* (flat noodles): wrapped around a wooden stick, the dough is then pulled off and cut into *stringhe* (strands) about the width of a finger.[42] These are the two fundamental ways of shaping pasta: roll out the dough and then cut it; extract directly from the dough some filaments or other shapes.

The term *macharoni* (macaroni), attested as early as the XI century,[43] initially indicated flour or semolina dumplings (*gnocchi*) cut from a rather thick dough. Their inclusion in the category of dried pasta was tied to practices like those documented by Maestro Martino: making them thinner or piercing them were ways of facilitating the drying, and it is certainly no coincidence that Martino himself recommends doing this. Sicilian macaroni, he writes, "must be dried in the sunlight" and that way "they will last two or three years."[44] Court cooking displays unexpected convergences with industrial food production practices, venturing into more systematic experimentation with an operating model—the drying of pasta—which had long been a part of domestic cooking, but on an occasional or periodic basis. This is another reason why the term "*macharoni*" would come to indicate dried pasta in general, even as it was used in a more specialized fashion to indicate the long and thin variety.

The *spagho* mentioned in the Sicilian macaroni recipe refers to the wire for piercing the dough, but another recipe for "*macharoni*," or "truly *tagliarini*" (thin-cut strips), which Maestro Martino dubs "a la zenovese" (Genoese) calls for cutting them "as thin as a *spagho*."[45] This is the first time that the word *spagho* appears in a gastronomic context. The road to *spaghetti* is now in sight, even though there will be a long wait (all the way to the mid-1800s) before we meet this term.[46] *Maccheroni* will remain for centuries—and it remains even today in Naples—the chosen word to refer to them.[47]

A New Category of Food

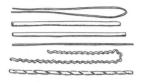

The coming together of all these experiences on the double track of domestic custom and industrial practices will bring to fruition in Italy an idea that previously had taken shape only in the Arabic[48] and—elsewhere and in a different way—the Chinese cultures of food.[49] This was the idea of pasta not just as one food product among many, a mere ingredient to be used in recipes of various kinds, but as a *genus* in and of itself, a new *category* of food,[50] simply called *pasta*. We see this toward the end of the Middle Ages, both in treatises on diet and in cookbooks.

Physicians are the first to take notice of the novelty, to catalogue all together the products that were gradually coming into being and to give them a collective name, in order to define some general rules of preparation and consumption useful for maintaining good health. New rules—just as the products were new—whose major concern (to which we will return further on) will be to counteract the "moist" and "viscous" nature of pasta.

The *Compendium de naturis et proprietatibus alimentorum* (Compendium of the Nature and Properties of Foods) by Barnaby da Reggio (1338) brings together under the denomination *tri* a series of dried pasta products known by different names depending on the local dialect:

tria in Ancona, *vermicelli* in Tuscany, *orati* in Bologna, *minutelli* in Venice, *fermentini* in Reggio Emilia, and *pancardelle* in Mantua . . . [51] In the next century, Benedetto Riguardati da Norcia writes of macaroni, lasagna, and other "pasta dishes" (*ferculis de pasta*).[52] In the Italian vulgate translation of Benedetto's compendium of dietetics, published in 1481 and attributed (wrongly) to the physician Ugo Benzi, the concept is rendered with the formula "manzare de pasta"[53] (pasta meals). Also in the XV century, the dietetic manual by Michele Savonarola cites together and puts on the same level "*lasagna, lasagnole, menudelli, tri,* and *nevole.*"[54]

It will take a bit longer for the concept of "pasta" to be used explicitly in cookbooks, although Maestro Martino tends to put macaroni, lasagna, vermicelli, and ravioli very close to one another in the order of his recipes. As Bruno Laurioux has observed,[55] the terminology used in cookbooks for these dishes remained in flux for a long time, indicating pasta that was fresh or dried, rolled or filled, and of various shapes and sizes. But that is exactly where the novelty lies: including differences under a shared terminology leads to equivocation and ambiguity, but at the same time it indicates a new way of perceiving these food preparations as making up an all-in-one. This will remain typical of the Italian culture and language: *pasta* is untranslatable in English or German, and in the principal Romance languages it is rendered in the plural, as in the French *pâtes* or the Spanish *pastas*. Only in Italian does the singular express the plurality of the experiences.

After the Medieval turning point, the "*minestre di pasta*" (pasta first courses or pasta meals) will be the locus *par excellence* of gastronomic diversification and, consequently, the symbol and metaphor of a culture, like Italy's, based on the diversity of local traditions. Around 1565, the variety of pasta dishes was expressed as follows by the botanist from the Marches, Costanzo Felici: "Either it comes in a thin and flat form like paper, or somewhat thicker, or it is made into a long and cylindrical shape with a hole in the middle, or it is pulled into thin filaments, which are either cut or strained into thin strings or small pieces. Of these varieties, you will hear various and different names, such as lasagna, pulled lassagnola, macaroni or cavadoli pulled into various shapes, strings, tagliatelli, vermicelli, granetti and other names . . ."[56]

How Do You Cook Pasta?

Boiling pasta in a pot of salted water is an operation that to a lot of people seems obvious, but in the history of cooking there is very little that is obvious, or maybe nothing.

I'll allow myself a personal memory. Some time ago, some American university students, whom I had asked to indicate what products they perceived as "typically" Italian, allotted first place to water. Right then and there, I thought they meant mineral water or bottled water, of which Italians are some of the world's greatest consumers. They explained to me, instead, that they were thinking of water for boiling pasta (not coincidentally, they had put salt in second place, which should have clued me in). Actually, this gesture is not automatically tied to cooking pasta, especially if you buy it already cooked or frozen, in which case your instrument becomes a frying pan or the oven, preferably a microwave. Gestures and ideas tied to different cultures, historically distant from the tradition of pasta? Perhaps. But we have already seen that there were centuries of uncertainty regarding the way to cook pasta. Boiled, sure, but also fried, steamed, baked, sautéed . . . Who *decided* and when that the best way was to boil it in a liquid? And that the liquid could be simple salted water (or possibly, and more appetizingly, broth)?

You might think it was just trial and error. By trying and trying again, you finally figure out what works better and what worse. But this empirical explanation is accompanied by a different one, of a theoretical nature. We find it in texts on dietetics, which for millennia have recommended "tempering" the qualities of foods, by balancing and adjusting the opposites on the two fundamental axes of hot/cold and dry/moist, the qualities that ancient Greek science had indicated as the constitutive elements of the universe and all things in it. A fundamental principle of the medical culture inaugurated by Hippocrates of Kos in the V-IV centuries BCE—and which was later dubbed "Galenic" because it was refined in the II century by Galen of Pergamon—was that of looking for the point of equilibrium in which opposites compensate for or correct each other. *Contraria contrariis curantur*, "opposites cure opposites" was the basic rule.

The first field of application for this rule was cooking, both in the choice of combinations (putting together ingredients with opposing qualities) and in cooking practices: roast moist ingredients to dry them; boil dry products to moisten them.[57] This was the scientific basis—confirmed by experience—that fostered the habit of cooking pasta in water, or in broth, or milk, to rehydrate a dehydrated product. Born as a response to the invention of dried pasta, over time the practice became general, expanding to lasagna and tortelli (filled pastas), which came less and less to be cooked in the oven or frying pans, as had often been proposed in medieval recipes. All pasta, even when it was fried, was subjected to a preliminary boiling. At the close of the XII century, the dictionary by Uguccione da Pisa explains the lemma *laganum* as "a genus of food which is first cooked in water, and then fried in oil."[58]

There remained just one problem. Once cooked, the pasta became soft, gluey, viscous. This "softness" was also appreciated, to the point that very long cooking times, on the order of hours, were recommended. Maestro Martino suggests cooking vermicelli "for the space of an hour," and Sicilian macaroni "for the space of two hours."[59] But this naturally led to the suggestion of a corrective measure, to temper the moistness that the pasta, if fresh, already possessed, or, if dried, had acquired, during the boiling. In all cases, the physicians—first in the Arab-Islamic world and later in Europe—recognized in *moistness* the main characteristic of pasta and suggested, to correct it, the use of *dried* ingredients such as pepper or other spices,[60] which, given their prohibitive cost, were one of the main symbols of social privilege.

This same principle gave scientific support to the combination of pasta and cheese, which encountered extraordinary success in cooking customs.

CHEESE ON MACARONI

It is hard to know if it was practice that supported theory, or vice versa. The most plausible explanation is that theory suggested practice, and then taste decreed its success. But we really cannot rule out that theory took note of established practices, justifying them *after the fact*. However you slice it, the history of pasta is tied with a double knot to the history of cheese—especially aged cheese, whose "dry" nature, in strict observance of the dietary rules, was thought to be ideal for balancing the "moist" nature of its companion.[61] Grating it fine (or shredding it into ribbons) favored its blending with the still boiling-hot pasta.

Benedetto Reguardati, the physician from Norcia who, as we have seen, was attentive to the *ferculis de pasta* as a new category of food, inserts his considerations on the matter in his chapter on cheese (*de caseo*): "For foods of a viscous humor, cheese is most suitable, and it is properly eaten with macaroni, lasagna, and [other] pasta dishes."[62] He is echoed by the XIV century *Liber de coquina:* "It is to be known that on lasagna and in *corzetti* (pasta circles cut from rolled dough) you must put a large amount of grated cheese": *debet poni magna quantitas casei gratati.*[63]

But which cheese? Dietetic manuals and cookbooks leave the choice open, respecting different tastes and habits. Cooks could use traditional cheeses, such as *cacio pecorino* made from sheep's milk, or innovative products, such as those that began to become popular in the middle centuries of the Middle Ages, in parallel with the development of cattle breeding. Of all of these cheeses, one was especially recommended: parmigiano—or piacentino, or lodigiano, or milanese, as were the names of the various kinds of "*grana*" that could be purchased in the cities of the Po Valley. Parmigiano and its siblings were born precisely in those years, between the XII and XIII centuries, in the large farms—often the properties of Cistercian monks—in which new experiments in zootechnics were first tried out, and which were frequented, as they took their herds to pasture, by shepherds from the nearly Alpine foothills. Alongside the consolidated practices of sheep grazing (and of wild pig breeding) new breeding establishments were promoted with the focus on cows— up to that time used almost exclusively for plowing—for the production of meat and milk. This production innovation led to the appearance on the market of cheeses made from cow's milk, which gradually took their place next to *pecorini* (sheep's milk cheeses).[64]

In the mid-1400s, the humanist Platina observed that there were now two varieties of cheese that "contend for first place in Italy": the Tuscan *marzolino* (pecorino) and the parmigiano from the cisalpine regions.[65] This judgment is repeated in 1471 in the *Summa lacticiniorum* by Pantaleone da Confienza—the oldest European treatise on dairy products—indicating the Florentine or marzolino and the piacentino or parmigiano as the most prestigious Italian cheeses (adding, in third place, the *robiola* cheeses of the Langhe area of Piedmont).[66]

Thanks to their reputation, the new products also became part of the dietary customs of the upper classes, who up to that time had been suspicious of cheese as an element of the poor diet of shepherds and peasants.[67] But it was not only a question of quality. What was decisive in the upward social mobility of cheese was the place that aged cheeses came to occupy in the gastronomic *system*— a coherent structure within which every product, every ingredient, plays a role and takes on *meaning*. In doing historical analysis, it is not particularly useful to concentrate on the experience of a specific product. Only the context, only the "dietary associations"—the felicitous expression of Fernand Braudel[68]—allow us to place those experiences, otherwise destined to dissolve into abstraction, within a historical framework.

The success of "grana" in all of its forms—and more generally the good fortune of hard cheeses—was their combination with pasta, which worked on the level of taste just as well as it did in dietetic theory. That is why the history of these two products has evolved hand-in-hand over the centuries. The evidence from cookbooks and culinary literature *always* points to cheese (preferably parmigiano) as the ideal condiment for pasta. *Numquam vidi hominem, qui ita libenter lagana cum caseo comederet sicut ipse*, or rather "I have never seen a man so happy to eat lasagna with cheese as that guy there."[69] This image of Friar Giovanni da Ravenna, sketched in the XIII century by the Franciscan Salimbene da Parma, is almost the archetype of a gastronomic choice of extraordinary and lasting success. Cheese on macaroni soon entered the world of Italian proverbs—and has never left it—to indicate an ideal combination, the perfect outcome of an enterprise, while *maccaron senza cascio* (macaroni without cheese) became the metaphor for imperfection—used as early as the 1500s by Pietro Aretino alongside equally dramatic absences of an essential element, such as *cocina senza cuoco* (kitchen without a cook) or *il mangier senza bere* (eating without drinking).[70]

Likewise, grated cheese yearned for nothing as much as pasta. In the mid-1300s a celebrated novella from Boccaccio's *Decameron* takes us—together with the ingenuous Calandrino—to the fabulous village of Bengodi, where food is guaranteed to all, in abundance and labor-free. Right in the center of town, "they had a mountain made entirely of grated parmesan cheese, where people did nothing but make gnocchi and ravioli that they cooked in capon broth. Then they would toss them down below, and the more you picked up the more you had."[71] (Translation Wayne A. Rebhorn.)

Bengodi is the fantastical country of Cockaigne, the land of plenty that appears in the utopian literature of half of Europe in the early Middle Ages. The mountain of parmigiano with macaroni and ravioli rolling down its slopes is its typically Italian variation, inaugurated by Boccaccio, carried on for centuries in our literature and later featured in prints and drawings.[72] In the modern era, macaroni would become something completely different from what Boccaccio had in mind, in all probability a cascade of gnocchi (in accordance with the oldest definition of the term, which works better than macaroni in this image of pieces of pasta in free fall down the mountainside). But the condiment would not change, certified by now as a *mark* of the Italian culinary identity.[73]

Another Way to Eat: The Fork

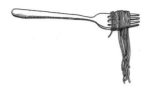

Dietary customs also have a strong relationship with eating tools, as demonstrated by the case of the fork; a new tool for a new food.

Until the second half of the Middle Ages, the typical tools for eating were the spoon, used as a vehicle for liquid foods, and the knife (most often collective) for cutting solid foods at the dinner table. With few exceptions, there was no specific piece of tableware for eating solid foods. Hands were thought to be more than sufficient—not least because they allowed for direct, immediate, *physical* contact with the food, something that was greatly appreciated, and, in Europe, well into the 1600 and 1700s, preferred to the "mediation" of the fork, with its unpleasant metallic taste.[74] In other parts of the world, this is still the rule. The first manuals of "good manners," which in Europe date back to the XIII-XIV centuries, delved extensively into the proper use of the hands (for example, suggesting not to use all five fingers to hold the food, but only three) while completely ignoring the fork.

The main exception was Italy, where use of the fork—or similar tools—makes a precocious appearance, not only (as one could imagine) in the exclusive circles of princely courts, but also in bourgeois society, and even among the plebeians. This happens because the fork is *functional*—almost necessary, one might say—in the consumption of pasta, which, as we have just seen, is normally dressed with cheese (and plenty of butter)[75] and served steaming hot. So served, pasta takes on two characteristics, slipperiness and heat, not well suited to the use of hands.

This is the reason that the fork comes to be used in Italy before the other European countries. At the end of its recipe for lasagna, the *Liber de coquina* takes pains to point out the convenience of bringing lasagna to the mouth with a *punctorio ligneo*, a wooden pointed instrument that was a sort of "prelude" to the fork.[76] Toward the end of the same century, an entertaining novella by Franco Sacchetti introduces the reader to a certain Noddo d'Andrea, pictured at table as he "begins to toss the macaroni, winds them up, and stuffs them in his mouth." Noddo was famous for the speed with which he managed to ingurgitate his food, even steaming hot. Indeed, when he had already swallowed six mouthfuls of those "boiling hot macaroni," his tablemate "still had her first mouthful on her fork."[77] This may be the earliest text—we are at the end of the XIV century—to use the term "maccheroni" to indicate, not medieval gnocchi, and not even pasta in general, but specifically spaghetti, which Noddo *winds up*, or twirls.

Evidence also comes from private documents, such as a curious inventory of the goods stolen by an armed band of thieves on the docks of the port of Cesenatico. Among the other merchandise, there is mention of fourteen dozen forks *ad comedendum macherones* (for eating macaroni).[78] The expression does not refer to a "specially" shaped fork used for that specific purpose. It simply

means that in those times forks were used—by definition—for eating pasta. Thus, their precocious appearance in Italy is a sign of the importance that pasta was
already assuming in the country's eating habits.

PASTA CHANGES ITS STATUS

In 1958, Emilio Sereni published a pioneering essay on the history of pasta, entitled *Note di storia dell'alimentazione nel Mezzogiorno: i napoletani da "mangiafoglia" a "mangiamaccheroni"* (Notes on the Dietary History of the South: The Neapolitans from "greens-eaters" to "macaroni-eaters"). Sereni's essay is a masterpiece of method, a "classic" that still has a lot to teach us. For one thing, it teaches us that the history of food is a complex field of study, which brings together economics and culture, technics and politics, material and imagination, and that all these elements contribute to the development of what Jean-Louis Flandrin called "structures of taste." *Structures* because the taste for food is not a gratuitous quirk, dependent on individual caprice, but a phenomenon rooted in precise historical experiences.

Indeed, Sereni sets out to understand *when, how, and why* the taste for macaroni got to be so prevalent in Naples as to justify the nickname "macaroni-eaters" by which Neapolitans have been known ever since the XVII century. By analyzing a vast range of sources, from archival documents to works of poetry and literature, Sereni showed that the same nickname, up to that time, was used as a label not for Neapolitans but for Sicilians—as we have already seen.[79] The reason for that we already know: Sicily had been, in the middle phase of the Middle Ages, the incubator of the culture of pasta—and particularly of dried pasta—in Italy. Then something happened.

Despite its growing expansion, pasta had still not become a *staple food*. In Naples, it was considered a luxury item, or at least, something that people could and should do without in hard times. A proclamation in 1509 prohibits the fabrication of dried pasta in times of war and famine, so as not to "waste" wheat.[80] But around 1630 things changed radically. The market of the city of Naples had been impoverished by frequent famines and by the incompetent Spanish administration. The supply of meat, until that time accessible even to the lower rungs of the social ladder, diminished drastically. The Neapolitans—traditionally known as "greens-eaters" because the "greens" (more precisely, cabbage and related vegetables) were, along with meat, the main supplement to bread in the daily diet—were forced to invent a new food regimen.

In the meantime, the two key machines of the pasta industry, attested in Italy from the XVI century,[81] had been introduced in Naples: the mixer, or mechanical dough kneader, inspired by the ones used in the textile industry to roll linen and hemp; and the press, inspired by the ones used to crush grapes, which pressed the pasta into the holes of a metallic extruder to obtain the desired shapes. The *contrivance for macaroni*, it was called by Cristoforo Messisbugo, chef and general superintendent of the Este court in Ferrara, in a cookbook published in 1549, the year after his death.[82]

Yet again we can observe a convergence of interests between the procedures for making pasta in the "domestic" sphere (to the extent we can use this expression for the large kitchens of noble courts) and in the manufacturing and industrial sector. In Naples, possession of a *contrivance* was an indispensable requirement for membership in the pasta-makers guild, the *Arte dei Vermicellari*.[83] The systematic adoption of these machines was the decisive step toward the large-scale production of pasta, based not on dough that was first rolled and then cut, but on the direct manipulation of the dough—which the *contrivance* allowed to be done much more efficiently and with less expenditure of energy.

Technological innovation led to a drastic drop in pasta production costs and its price to the consumer. Macaroni was thus "promoted" to the staple food of Neapolitans, and the pasta/cheese duo replaced the cabbage/meat duo. So that's why, as early as the XVII century, the epithet "macaroni-eaters" started being attributed to Neapolitans.[84]

Over the course of these developments, the status of pasta changed. Up to that time, though it had carved out an important place for itself in the diet (and in the dreams of the popular classes; as in the land of Bengodi), it had never been a stable part of the daily diet, whose main players were bread, polenta, soup, and boiled vegetables. When it came to the course offerings of *haute cuisine*, however, pasta was mostly relegated to an accessory role, as a side dish for meats or fish—a practice still common in the culinary cultures north of the Alps, regarded as a scandal by many Italians but actually a return to our oldest gastronomic traditions. The XIV century *Liber de coquina* suggests serving Genoese pasta (*tria ianuensi*) "with capons, eggs, and any kind of meat."[85] Bartolomeo Scappi, the most renowned Italian chef of the XVI century, records recipes such as "boiled kneaded capons topped with lasagne," "boiled large stuffed geese alla Lombarda, topped with annolini," "stewed local chicken topped with Neapolitan macaroni," and so on.[86]

From the XVII century on, the grammar of the Neapolitan diet was different, with pasta winning, for the first time, the leading role. Macaroni would become the street food par excellence of the popular neighborhoods, and pasta stands would become places of entertainment for gentlemen visiting the city.

Al Dente

A l dente is the title of a recent book by Fabio Parasecoli, devoted to the history of food in Italy.[87] This untranslatable expression (indeed, English speakers generally use the Italian phrase, literally "to the tooth") evokes in a synthetic fashion an essential element of Italian gastronomic culture, pasta, and at the same time, the proper way to cook it: not too long, in order to keep it firm to the bite.

Nevertheless, medieval and Renaissance cookbooks recommended cooking pasta a long time, for a number of minutes that today would leave us aghast. "These macaroni want to boil for the space of two hours," Maestro Martino prescribes in his recipe for Sicilian macaroni. The indication was apparently susceptible to rather significant variations, with another manuscript of the same book reducing the cooking time to "one hour gently gently" and still another takes it down to half an hour—while adding, however, that in principle "all pasta wants to be well cooked."[88] Bartolomeo Scappi, in the 1500s, also suggests prolonged cooking. For his "Romanesque macaroni dish" he advises pre-cooking in boiling water for half an hour, then "taste them to see if they are tender, and if not, keep them at a boil until they are well cooked." That's not all. At this point, the pasta is put onto a plate, disposed on three layers each topped with grated cheese, sugar, and cinnamon, then the whole thing is covered with an overturned plate and left to stew on the hot coals, or in the oven, for another half hour.[89]

It is only in the XVII century that things seem to change. Perhaps the first sign of change came from Giovanni Del Turco, Florentine musician and gastronome, who in his cookbook finds "appropriate" a cooking time for macaroni that is not too long, and followed by an immediate cold-water rinse "that will make the pasta stiff and firm."[90] But the taste for quick cooking seems to come to the fore only for pasta that is fresh and thin, such as *tagliolini*, which on the cusp of the XVII century the Neapolitan Antonio Latini recommends cooking only as long as necessary "because being thin they want little cooking."[91]

The extension of the practice, even for kinds of dried pasta such as spaghetti, probably begins in Naples, among the pasta stands set up along the streets for a quick made-to-order meal, probably the ideal place and situation for appreciating the texture and consistency of the product.[92] By 1839, when Ippolito Cavalcanti, Duke of Buonvicino, publishes the second edition of his Neapolitan cookbook, with a new appendix in dialect on "homestyle cooking", he takes the short cooking time for granted: "make sure you cook the macaroni *vierd, vierd*" (green, green, that is, very firm), and "when you think they're cooked, take the pot off the fire right away and toss in a mug of cold water."[93] The same splash of water suggested by Del Turco.

Toward the end of the XIX century, Pellegrino Artusi accepts this practice and proposes it to Italians generally: "As for the macaroni themselves," he writes, "the Neapolitans recommend that they should be boiled in a large pot, with lots of water, and not cooked too long."[94] The father of modern Italian cooking also looks for a dietetic justification, observing that, remaining hard, the macaroni must be chewed longer before swallowing, so they become more digestible. In any case, this is the line that will have the most success in Italy, albeit intermittently and with some variation.

Not coincidentally, the habit of cooking pasta until it is softened, or to *scuocerla* (overcook it), as Italians like to say, has remained alive where it has preserved its ancient function as a side dish. The two things go hand in hand, and so we can only deduce that it was the liberation of pasta, its change in status from a supporting to a leading role, that suggested giving it more consistency, to give it a better and longer lasting taste.

WE ARE WHAT WE EAT

Food is an extraordinary mark of identity, both for the principle of incorporation inherent in the action of eating, and for the extra-nutritional, symbolic values that are attached to the culture of food in all societies. That is why food is such a powerful sign of belonging to a community; that is why gastronomical epithets are so widespread, at times in a tone of proud self-representation, at times in a tone of derision, to ridicule others—no matter who they are. We have gotten a glance of this in the case of the "macaroni-eater" epithet used, first, to tease Sicilians and then, starting with the XVII-XVIII centuries, as the emblem of the new culinary identity developed in Naples. By the 1800s, "macaroni" had become synonymous with Naples, in literary representations as well as in the collective imagination, and it is curious that at the time of Italian political unification the conquest of Naples could be represented as a macaroni feast—and the conquest of Sicily as a celebratory orange binge.

On 26 July 1860, upon completion of the occupation of Sicily and awaiting the arrival of Garibaldi's troops on the mainland, Camillo Cavour writes to the Piedmontese ambassador in Paris: "The oranges are already on our table and we have decided to eat them. As for the mainland, it is better to wait, because the macaroni are still cooking." On

7 November Garibaldi enters Naples and Cavour writes: "The macaroni are done and we are going to eat them." Such expressions could lend themselves to malicious comments (the North that eats the South). But they must also be interpreted—as Franco La Cecla suggests—as a reflection of the desire on the part of Piedmont's political leadership to legitimize its role as the guarantor of the interests and traditions of all, in the delicate conclusive moment of the country's unification. To that end, Cavour and his administration take measures directed at the collective imagination, in addition to more strictly political programs, to bring about a sort of "southernization" of the subalpine identity. In this operation, symbolic foods are, as always, decisive. To eat macaroni is to share a culture, transforming the symbol of Naples (and by extension, the whole Kingdom of the Two Sicilies) into a symbol of the nation. The "national revolution," to the extent that it means the "ingestion of the South on the part of the North," is also a revolution of the gastronomic image, which—according to La Cecla—"*pulls farther north* the Mediterranean blanket, of which macaroni are an essential element."[95]

In the meantime, the "Neapolitan" model spread throughout the Italian South, where initially it had interested only the urban and coastal areas, more tied to the logic and mechanisms of the food market. In the rural regions of the interior, pasta remained for a long time a food of the rich, consumed only occasionally by the poor, so much so that, as Vito Teti has observed, even at the start of the XX century, Parliamentary investigations gathered testimony that defined macaroni as "a meal fit for a King."[96] Already at the time of unification, however, the moniker "macaroni-eaters" had taken on a wider application, representing not only Neapolitans, but Southerners in general—while the politico-cultural project of the Savoy dynasty meant to confer upon it a still broader sense of *Italianness*.

The elaboration of this image also owed a lot to the phenomenon of emigration, the dramatic exodus that, in the closing decades of the XIX century, scattered throughout Europe and the Americas millions of Italians in search of work and food. More typical of the regions of the South, where most of the emigrants left from, the consumption of pasta was recognized as a distinctive element of Italian "diversity." This stereotype, as usually happens, was constructed by *others* to identify and ridicule the new arrivals and their strange customs. Italian emigrants in America were called *macaroni*. In France they were called *spaghetti*, with the accent on the i.

But this same stereotype also functioned as an element of internal cohesion. The *dream* of eating pasta—so it had remained for many of the Italians who were forced to leave their homeland—was more likely to come true beyond the Alps and especially in America. Newfound work brought more resources to families and increased their chances of access to the pasta market, which crossed the ocean for the very purpose of continuing that custom and responding to the unsatisfied emigrant demand. Land of abundance, a "mardi gras come true" that finally made it possible to eat pasta—and meat—on a daily basis, America made a decisive contribution to the consolidation of the stereotype of Italians as macaroni-eaters, and in many cases it was the place where it actually played out. A lot of Southern peasants became macaroni-eaters only after emigrating to America.[97]

White and Red

Is *amatriciana* sauce white or red?

The tomato is one of those things that divides the world in two, and since white has become "old style," it is not hard to deduce that in the history of gastronomy there is a *before* and an *after* the introduction of the tomato. But the process has been rather long and full of twists and turns, and it is not possible to mark an exact point on the time line that divides the two periods.

For centuries, pasta was rigorously served white. Cheese (with the addition of butter and spices for those who could afford them) was its most customary condiment. The use of lard and, sometimes, oil has also been attested. But the color was always white. That changed with the arrival of tomato sauce, but it arrived late, not before the 1800s. Goethe, who was in Naples in 1787, notes that "the macaroni [. . .] are cooked simply in water and are dressed with grated cheese."[98] At that time, the tomato had been known for centuries, and we have to explain not only what factors led to its finally being used but also why it took so long.

Original to the western coasts of South America, where it still grows wild, the tomato enjoyed an extraordinary success among the Maya and the Aztecs. It was in Mexico that it met up with the Spaniards of Hernán Cortés, when they occupied the country between 1519 and 1521. It was immediately taken to Spain and that's how the tomato came to be grafted onto the gastronomic culture of Italy. Naturalists and botanists are the first to mention it, starting with Pietro Andrea Mattioli (1544) who cites it in his commentary on the pharmacological text of Pedacio Dioscoride.[99] Of these "new plants just arrived in Italy," Mattioli describes the appearance and color, red or golden, explaining that they can be sliced and cooked like eggplant, that is, in a frying pan, and dressed with salt, olive oil, and black pepper. Just ten years later, in a new edition of the book, he would give these plants a name, "pomi d'oro" (golden pomes), which would become the established name in Italian (while Spanish and the other major European languages would use names derived from the Aztec *tomatl*).

Tomatoes, then, are treated *like eggplants*. This association, justified on the botanical level by their common belonging to the Solanaceae family, would be adopted by subsequent writers and it would not have a positive influence on the image of the tomato, given the prejudices against the eggplant, known in Italian as *melanzana* or *mela* (apple) *insana* (insane or unhealthy).[100] Pietro Antonio Michiel goes so far as to classify these "pomes from Peru" as a variety of eggplant and repeats, like Mattioli, that they are to be cooked in a frying pan "with butter or oil" but that they are "harmful and noxious"; their very odor causes "torment to the eyes and the head."[101] Castore Durante (1585) also defines tomatoes as a "kind of eggplant" and reiterates that they "give little and bad nourishment."[102] Again, in 1628, the Paduan physician Giovanni Domenico Sala would describe tomatoes and eggplant alike as

"strange and horrible things" that "a few imprudent people" are willing to eat.[103]

But these were judgments and prejudices of physicians.
In everyday life, these "impudent people" must not have
been so rare: "gluttonous and greedy for new things"—as
they were defined by Costanzo Felice in the mid-
1500s[104]—they are found not only among the modern
habitués of trendy restaurants and counterculture food
boutiques, but also among their Renaissance era (and
medieval and ancient) ancestors, who put curiosity above
diffidence. They also tried, no doubt, to find a point of
compromise with dietetic recommendations. If the tomato
was so intrinsically "cold" and "moist," as it was described
by the medical literature—based on the reigning Galenic
theory of the four qualities—then frying it in a pan and
dressing it with salt and pepper (as did the "gluttons" of
Costanzo Felici and the others we have mentioned) were
so many ways of warming and drying it, so as to render it,
so to speak, dietetically correct.

It is true, therefore, that for a long time the tomato
remained a botanical curiosity, a plant for a medicinal garden, used, perhaps for ornamental purposes: "it is not
good to eat but you can try keeping some just for beauty,"
writes the Florentine agronomist Giovanvettorio Soderini,
on the eve of the XVI century.[105] But this did not exclude
prudent experimentation. From this point of view as well,
the decisive factor was Italy's relationship with Spain, from
where Italians had imported their first tomatoes in the
form of seeds and plants. In 1548, Cosimo de' Medici
received a basket of tomatoes from the Florentine gardens
of Torre del Gallo, and this is the first evidence from the
"field" of an Italian interest for the new plant.[106] But at this

point we mustn't forget Cosimo's ties with Spain, activated through his wife Eleonore of Toledo, who shipped products to Spain from her holdings in Tuscany and, presumably, had imported the tomatoes from Spain.

The Spanish imprint on the tomato was to shift from the botanical and horticultural level to the gastronomical level, when—during the XVII century—it would make its entrance into Italian cooking. To do this, it would have to carve out a place for itself in a centuries-old category of food, sauces, that was an essential part of ancient, medieval, Renaissance, and baroque cooking.

Spanish Tomato Sauce

In the system of traditional cooking, no dish, whether meat, or fish, or vegetable, or pasta, was exempt from being accompanied by a sauce, selected each time from a vast repertory, to which cookbooks, like dietary manuals, devoted ample chapters. The systematic use of *flavors*—such were called accompanying sauces—allowed cooks to "temper" and "correct" any putative nutritional imbalances in their dishes, in accordance with criteria and methods that we have already explained. Sauces were used to confer on a dish certain *qualities* and especially *flavor*, two properties of pre-modern culinary culture that were strictly tied to each other, given the belief that flavor was the perceptible form of a food's quality. Furthermore, sauces gratified the eye, adding a wide variety of *colors*— and at this point it is well to recall that, in the ancient and medieval traditions, colors and flavors moved in parallel, being endowed with precise correspondences, and both of them expressing the quality of the material. With regard to color (not yet, for the moment, flavor), this idea has been re-proposed in recent years by dietary science, which, today, recommends favoring foods of certain colors because they are particularly rich in nutritional elements.

Let's get back to our tomato. The properties of the new product included, not least among them, the capacity to add red to the palette of colors of traditional sauces. Tomato sauce enters European cookbooks in the XVII century, and it is often denominated "Spanish"—for reasons that are not hard to understand.

The first to talk about this sauce, reporting on food customs observed in Mexico, had been Francisco Hernández, physician at the court of Philip II and "chief physician of all the Indies." During a long research trip to the New World (1570-77), he sent back to the king sixteen volumes with descriptions of American plants and their medical and gastronomical uses. Digested in various forms from the original Latin or from the Spanish translation, these descriptions circulated in Europe and primarily in Italy, where Hernández's work was published in Latin in 1628, and later in Italian. The volume includes a description of a delicious sauce or *intinctus* (dip) that "is prepared from sliced tomatoes and chili pepper, which enriches the flavor or almost all dishes and almost all foods, and reawakens the appetite."[107]

This is the Mexican tradition which, by way of Spain, arrives in Italy—an Italy that, in the XVII century, was governed or controlled by Madrid. The first recipe appears in the *Scalco alla moderna* (The Modern Steward) by Antonio Latini (1692), a figure who was completely "integrated" in the world of Spanish power. Born in the Marches, he worked as a steward for various families before landing in the court of Esteban Carrillo y Salcedo, Spanish grandee and regent of the vice-realm of Naples, who named him a "Knight of the Golden Spur" and Count Palatine. In his cookbook, all of the recipes that feature the tomato are dubbed "alla spagnola" (Spanish style). This is his recipe for tomato sauce "alla spagnola":

Take some ripe tomatoes, toasted over the wood fire and skinned. Dice them fine with a knife, add some diced onion, chili pepper (*peparolo*) if you wish, also diced, a pinch of thyme (*serpyllum*). Mix everything together and dress with salt, oil, and vinegar "which will make a tasty sauce for boiled meat, or for other things."[108]

As an accompaniment to boiled meat, "or other things," the red sauce was fully welcomed into Italian cooking of the 1700 and 1800s. Its "reduction" to a sauce found the tomato a suitable place in the gastronomic system, sidestepping all discussion. In parallel with this success there was a change, or rather a complete reversal, of the traditional sentiments and age-old diffidence of physicians with respect to the tomato—not least because, in the meantime, Galenic medicine had marked time in the face of the advance of a new science and new interpretive paradigms, tied more to chemistry than physics. In his multifaceted activity as chef, philosopher, and man of letters, Vincenzo Corrado, refined interpreter of XVIII century Neapolitan culture, has only good things to say about tomatoes, to which he devotes a special chapter in his treatise *Del cibo pitagorico* (On Pythagorean Food, 1781), that is, on the vegetarian diet.

Corrado writes that, if you listen to the doctors, tomatoes "do a lot, with their acidic juice, to facilitate digestion, particularly during their summer season, during which, overcome by the heat, man's stomach is relaxed and nauseous."[109] The reference to the *acidic juice* said to favor digestion supposes the overcoming of the medieval theorem that represented digestion as a cooking process (the stomach as a "pot" in which food cooked) and seems to allude to new "chemical" interpretations that were starting to become accepted. In any case, it is no longer heat that is sought, as an agent of the presumed digestive cooking, but rather acid to "dissolve" the nutritive principles.

Corrado also gives us, in his *Cuoco galante* (Gentleman Chef, 1773), a recipe for "tomato sauce" (to boil in mutton gravy to then be served with the mutton itself) that, compared to Latini's prototype, replaces the onion with garlic cloves, the thyme with rue and pennyroyal, and gets rid of the vinegar. It retains, however, the red chili pepper ("peparolo rosso"), companion par excellence of the tomato.[110]

Up to this point, our sauce has not yet encountered spaghetti.

A Felicitous Encounter

Once again, it was Naples where, in the first half of the XIX century, the marriage between pasta and the tomato was held—even though, unexpectedly, the first news of the event arrived from France. In 1807, the *Almanach des gourmands* by Grimod de La Reynière—a cult book in the history of gastronomy—explained that tomatoes could sometimes take the place of cheese as a condiment for vermicelli.[111] This would contribute "a very pleasant acidity that is generally appreciated by those who have developed the habit." This is the same *acidity* alluded to by Vincenzo Corrado, represented here as a new practice, and anyway not taken for granted.

We do not know if Grimod was referring to customs learned in Italy. In any case, everything indicates Naples as the place of the first experiments with tomato sauce on pasta (not, however, *in place of* cheese, as suggested by Grimod, but *in addition to* cheese). Already in 1781, Corrado himself had asserted that this "universal sauce" could be employed in "infinite dressings," lending itself "to meats, fish, eggs, *pastas*, and greens."[112] In 1807 (the same year as Grimod's account) a Neapolitan book of *Cucina casareccia* (Home Cooking), signed only with the initials M.F., proposed "maccheroni alla napoletana" dressed—or better, "loaded"—with aged cheese and grated *caciocavallo*, then served "with a good ragù gravy, in which the tomatoes, or tomato paste, have already been cooked."[113] An authoritative source, which allows us to date at least to this period the custom of *conserving* tomatoes in tomato paste, a domestic practice that in the decades to come would become a powerhouse of the Italian canning industry.

The gravy alluded to in the cookbook is the typical Neapolitan ragù, for which M.F. gives the recipe, recommending the use of larded beef or veal, stuck with cloves and cooked in a casserole with a little water (or broth) after having sautéed in the same pot onions, ham, lard, herbs, salt, and pepper. Possible addition, tomato: the ragù "will be better, if you also sauté some tomatoes in season, but after removing the skins," and perhaps adding a glass of good wine and "a healthy dose of rosemary."[114]

"Where is the cooking of the people in this *Cucina casareccia*?" wonders Lejla Mancusi Sorrentino, who had seen to the publication of the cookbook. "M.F.'s macaroni are not proletarian macaroni, but noble macaroni, surrounded with aristocratic recipes, rich in seasoning, refined in their presentation, and delicately flavored."[115] True. M.F.'s macaroni casserole is a sumptuous triumph,[116] and even the macaroni in veal ragù doesn't seem to be affordable for everybody. However, it is also true that we are talking about the aristocratic interpretation of a culinary culture, which, in early XIX century Naples, is perceived as "popular." Even and perhaps especially in its tomato variation, which, not coincidentally, is included in the aristocrats' ragù only as an option, albeit an ameliorative one (a choice can be "popular" but tasty just the same).

This is confirmed by the already-cited recipe of Ippolito Cavalcanti, who in *Cucina teorico-pratica* (Cooking theory and practice), published in Naples in 1837, makes no mention of pasta with tomato sauce. He includes it, however, two years later, in the second edition of the book, enriched with an appendix on popular cooking (evoked, as we have already seen, in the language of the people: dialect). In so doing, the titled gentleman underlines the strongly popular character of this new dietary custom, which, however, in accordance with a typically Neapolitan (but, I would say, Italian)[117] practice, does not take long to become the patrimony of the entire community.

In this *Cucina casareccia in dialetto napoletano*, the association pasta/tomato is signaled not in a recipe for macaroni but in the recipe for tomato sauce (*sauza de pommadore*). The sauce is made from crushed ripe and deseeded tomatoes, placed to cook in a casserole together with their juice (*acquiccia*) and stirred continuously until, once cooked, they will be milled and cooked down *ncoppa a lo fuoco* (over the fire). At the end, salt and pepper are added and the sauce is ready, very simple and truly "popular."

Now it's time to choose the fat to flavor the sauce. It depends, according to Cavalcanti, on what the sauce will be used for: "*p'acconcià li* maccaruni" (to dress macaroni) or boiled meat, eggs, chicken, or fish? For meat, fish, and eggs, "a little butter will be good"; for pasta, however, better to add "nzogna"[118] (lard or tallow). The Mediterranean diet was yet to be invented.

In any case, the pasta/tomato association has by now entered into common use, even if—in Naples and elsewhere—the centuries-old tradition that calls for spaghetti and all kinds of pasta to be dressed first of all with cheese, or better yet, with *lots* of cheeses, as recommended by Cavalcanti himself in his macaroni recipe, remains alive. The ideal is to drain the pasta immediately "coating it with aged cheese, and provola cheese, and any other kinds of cheese, the more the better." The more kinds of cheese you use, the better the taste of the macaroni. This continues to be the standard preparation, but "they can also be prepared with tomato sauce."[119]

In a couple of generations, the practice is consolidated. According to a study conducted in 1863 by two Neapolitan physicians, tomatoes "are the usual condiment for macaroni and not a day goes by without them appearing on the dinner table of the middle class."[120] But their common touch still prevails. In her *Il Ventre di Napoli* (The Belly of Naples, 1884), Matilde Sarao writes, "all the streets in the four lower class neighborhoods have one of these taverns that have their cauldrons set up in the open-air taverns where cauldrons of macaroni are always boiling and pots of tomato sauce are always bubbling, mountains of grated cheese . . ." It's the Land of Cockaigne (after which Serao will entitle one of her novels a few years later) become reality, with the added extra of tomato sauce.

Thirty years after the establishment of the Kingdom of Italy, Pellegrino Artusi published the first edition of *La scienza in cucina and l'arte di mangier bene* (Science in the Kitchen and the Art of Eating Well), the book that is the keystone of modern Italian cooking. Bringing together the recipes and culinary practices of upper class families throughout Italy, and presenting them in polished Italian, the book paves the way to the construction of a shared heritage. Over the course of the XX century, even the urban and rural working classes would draw on this heritage, recognizing in it important traces of their own culture filtered through the mediation of upper class tastes.[121] It would be Artusi who would spread throughout the country the "Southern" custom of dressing pasta with tomato sauce, the recipe for which is introduced by the curious anecdote about a priest in Romagna "who stuck his nose into everything, and busy-bodied his way into families, trying to interfere in every domestic matter." For this reason, "popular wit dubbed him *Don Pomodoro* (Father Tomato), since tomatoes are also ubiquitous. And therefore it is very helpful to know how to make a good tomato sauce." The sauce, seasoned with onion, garlic, celery, basil, parsley, olive oil, salt, and pepper, will lend itself "to innumerable uses, as I shall indicate in due course." It will be good with boiled meat (a classic pairing, suggested two centuries earlier by Antonio Latini), but above all it will be "excellent when served with cheese and butter on pasta."[122]

Later, on the cusp of the XX century, Artusi *added* tomato sauce to pasta dishes already dressed with cheese and butter, as in the most established Italian tradition (at least for the upper-middle and upper classes, since the lower classes could only afford lard). Only in the XX century would the roles tend to be reversed, when it would be the cheese that would be added after the tomato sauce, with which the spaghetti or other types of pasta would already be drenched.

A Spice for Everyone

L ike all varieties of peppers, the chili pepper comes from America, too. Its success in the Old World, where it rapidly acclimatized, was due to the ease with which it managed to insert itself into the gastronomic system. Chilis became a feature of both *haute cuisine*, which loved strong and spicy flavors, and popular cooking, which had been waiting for centuries—perhaps unconsciously—to be able to afford such flavors, traditionally perceived as a class privilege, a sign of exclusive social status. This new spice, hot, even burning hot, had the unusual advantage that it could be grown *in loco*. As noted in 1569 by Nicolò Monardes, Indian spices "cost many ducats" while the chili pepper "costs nothing but to plant it."[123] So, the chili pepper made a breach even in the culinary habits of farm families, or at least it was accessible at relatively low cost.

This (along with the decline in prices for Indian spices, brought about by the opening of new commercial routes by European sea captains and merchants) was one of the factors that accounted for a progressive exit of hot spices from upper class dinner tables, given that pleasures that are overly shared rapidly lose their charm.[124] From the XVII-XVIII centuries, the rich looked for other ways to express their diversity at table.[125]

The chili pepper plant and seeds were brought to the Old Continent in 1494 by Diego Álvarez Chanca, who sailed with Columbus on his second voyage to the Americas. The Inca-speaking populations called it *axì*, and Aztec-speakers called it *chili*. In 1535, Gonzalo Ferdinando de Oviedo recorded an accurate description of it, highlighting how the "Indians" used the fruit of this plant "instead of pepper," cultivating it and caring for it with great attention because "they eat it continuously with fish and other dishes of theirs." But there was also careful attention on the part of the European explorers: "it is just as pleasing to the taste of Christians as to that of the Indians," because in effect, "*asci* goes better with meat and fish than does good old pepper." And they "have already taken some to Spain as a good spice, and it is very salutary, and the people who use it are happy with it, so they send merchants and other people from Europe to bring some back here."[126]

The success of "Indian pepper" in Spain and Italy was immediate. In 1569, the already-cited Monardes writes that "in all of Spain there is no field nor vegetable garden nor vase that does not have some of it planted," and "it is used in all condiments and stews, because it tastes better than common pepper."[127] "By now it is common knowledge for everybody," Pietro Andrea Mattioli wrote in 1568.[128]

The chili pepper also made a precocious entry into tomato sauce. We have seen it all the way from the first recipe for the sauce, proposed in 1628 by the Spaniard Francisco Hernández.[129] Similarly, the first Italian recipe for "Spanish style" tomato sauce, dated 1692 and signed by Antonio Latini, calls for the use of *peparolo*.[130] It would seem, therefore, that this pairing was not coincidental but in some way primary to tomato sauce itself. Not without, perhaps, some dietary considerations. Associating the two products was perfectly in line with the traditional paradigm of medical science, given that the pairing brought together the "cold" quality of the tomato and the "hot" quality of the new spice. The pairing must have been tried out in aristocratic circles, both Spanish and Italian, and then it became a common heritage.

The increasing "popular" characterization of the chili pepper explains the prudence with which cookbooks of the 1700 and 1800s propose its use. Although including it in various recipes, Vincenzo Corrado, in his book *Cibo pitagorico* (1781), defines *peparoli* as "vulgar rustic food," having become "well-liked by many" and particularly by his fellow Neapolitans, "the inhabitants of the wandering Sebeto [the river that flowed through Naples in Greek times] who eat them, fried while they are still green, and sprinkle them with salt, or else grilled on the wood fire, and dressed with salt and olive oil."[131] Vincenzo Agnoletti (1803) specifies that the pepper, in all its variations, "is never served at elegant tables."[132]

The chili pepper, alone or added to tomato sauce (and, therefore, at some point combined with spaghetti) has by now become a standard of popular cooking.

OLIVE OIL AND THE INVENTION OF THE MEDITERRANEAN DIET

It was the American physician Ancel Keys, the inventor of the "K ration" distributed to American GIs during World War II, who deduced the advantages of a diet poor in meat and animal fat, like the one he encountered in the southern regions of Italy.

At this point we are in the 1950s, when the idea of a "Mediterranean diet," useful for good health and satisfying to the taste, was just beginning to take shape.[133] The primary ingredients of this diet, which was declared by UNESCO in 2010 part of the "intangible cultural heritage of humanity," are ways of living, the appreciation of conviviality, a harmonic relationship with yourself and others, with the rhythms of nature. When the world *diàita* first appeared in ancient Greek, it meant precisely this: the whole set of actions and mental attitudes that give shape to the "regimen" of daily life. Food is an essential part of this "regimen" but it is no coincidence that UNESCO classifies this and other cultural achievements as our *intangible* heritage.

It is stretching the point, therefore, to attribute to this designation the promotion of this or that food *product*— such as olive oil, or rather extra virgin olive oil, as it has come to be called to reinforce its position in the market. (The name is part of a strategy whose importance for the protection of a product always at risk of imitation we will not deny, but which has no significance for historical analysis.) Nevertheless, when it comes to the "Mediterranean diet," it is precisely this product—together with pasta, the tomato, and its other companions of adventure—that plays a central role in the collective imagination.

But olive oil has become an item of generalized use only in the last few decades, thanks to an extraordinary growth in production and greater commercial availability, which have gone hand in hand with the renewed prestige of this product and the dominant role it has taken on in the scale of food values. But it has also benefitted from the growing interest in dietary health which, starting with Ancel Keys, has identified it as an excellent antidote for cardiovascular risk.

Olive oil, to be sure, has an age-old history. It has been a distinctive element of Mediterranean culture for millennia. The oldest text in world literature—the Sumerian *Epic of Gilgamesh*, written 4,500 years ago on a clay tablet—represents it as an identifying sign of the process of civilization, along with bread and beer (that which humanity *creates* with intelligence and labor, by becoming farmers and learning to transform the world).[134] But in the story of Gilgamesh, which represents bread and beer as the food and drink of civilized man, oil is used as a body ointment. It is above all a cosmetic: a function it continued to have in the Greek and Roman world, even as it entered into use as a food, as a condiment, and as a cooking medium. The cuisine of ancient peoples was truly an oil cuisine, but with important geographical and social limitations. Outside of its production zone, actually rather small, olive oil was rare, costly, and a luxury of the few. To be sure, Apicius (the refined gourmet of the I century who is the presumed author of *De re coquinaria*—On the Subject of Cooking) knows olive oil only as a fatty condiment and cooking liquid. Nevertheless, behind him there was a whole world of peasants and shepherds, who were accustomed to using animal fat—mainly pork fat and lard—to flavor their dishes.[135]

This situation persisted and was accentuated in the Middle Ages, when the spread of "Barbarian" cultural models had the effect, on the economic and dietary fronts, of renewed prestige for livestock raising and the food products that derived from it, first among them pork and pork fat.[136] To be sure, in that same period, the dietary rules imposed by the Christian Church provided for abstinence from meat and animal fats for a substantial number of days and periods throughout the year.[137] With such limitations, the use of oil became practically an *obligation* throughout the Christian world.[138] But not necessarily olive oil. On the contrary, the Middle Ages were the epoch par excellence of seed oils, obtained from all kinds of different plants (above all, walnuts) given the persistent difficulty of procuring *that* kind of oil.[139]

For dressing salad greens, for cooking fish and vegetables, that is, "low-fat" foods, medieval cooks were "forced" to use oil. But when the calendar permitted, they used something else: lard, which was still the most common and most "popular" resource. Butter, whose use in Italy began to expand from the XII-XIII centuries with the increase in cattle breeding, established itself as a luxury product which, at some point—with the multiplication of papal dispensations—could also replace oil on days of abstinence.[140]

Toward the end of the Middle Ages, when pasta was beginning to come into its own as a distinctive dish of Italian cooking, butter was always used to enrich the cheese in recipes destined for wealthy dinner tables. For Maestro Martino it was the rule: Sicilian macaroni, he wrote, as soon as they are removed from the pot, must be arranged on platters "with ample amounts of grated cheese, *fresh butter,* and sweet spices."[141] This combination would be confirmed in the cooking of noble courts in the 1500s, and it is ubiquitous in the literature. In the mid-1500s, the *Commentario delle più notabili et mostruose cose d'Italia* (Commentary on the most noble and monstrous things of Italy), by Ortensio Lando—which includes a sort of gastronomic journey in Italy from South to North—explains that Sicilian macaroni "are usually cooked together with capon fat and fresh cheeses, *dripping with butter* and milk *on all sides.*"[142] A late sixteenth century novella by Celio Malespini includes a scene with a group of Venetian gentlemen savoring macaroni in Messina, dressed "with more than twenty-five pounds of parmigiano cheese, and six to eight caciocavalli, and endless spices: sugar, cinnamon, and *and so much butter they were swimming in it.*"[143]

The popular imagination doesn't take long to embrace this standard, and the iconography of the 1600 and 1700s of the Land of Cockaigne places a large lake of butter at the base of the mountain of cheese, gathering in the macaroni in free fall.[144] A dream, for the great majority. The alternative was to content yourself with pork fat, the age-old *leitmotiv* of peasant cooking.

Until just the other day, the lard of the poor and the butter of the rich (or of popular dreams) were the ideal accompaniment for our spaghetti. Dressing them with olive oil—or dressing tomato sauce with olive oil—was a possible option. In the mid-1500s, Costanzo Felici does not rule out the use of olive oil (or walnut or almond oil) on pasta, but its association with pepper "and other spices" seems to indicate a socially restricted custom.[145] At the end of the 1600s, Antonio Latini puts olive oil in his (the first in Italy) recipe for tomato sauce, but this was still an elite preparation, invented for aristocratic courts.[146]

In the *home cooking* appendix to his 1839 Neapolitan cookbook, Ippolito Cavalcanti is explicit in defining the social status of cooking fats, distinguishing a "noble" tomato sauce, good for accompanying meat and fish, from a "popular" sauce destined for pasta. For the first, he recommends butter, for the second, lard.[147] To be sure, this sauce "excellent for blending with vermicelli," could be enriched with olive oil. In this way, the pasta would come out "even better and tastier." But it is a variation that seems to be reserved for the few. The first choice, the really "popular" one, is lard, which turns up in the recipe for *"viermicielli co le pomodoro"* (vermicelli with tomato sauce), where the sauce is thickened and flavored, before being poured over the pasta, with an amount of *"nzogna"* (lard) equal to one-third of its volume.[148]

Lard is not absent from the section of his cookbook that Ippolito Cavalcanti writes in Italian and devotes to noble cooking. There, however, the prevailing cooking fat is butter—there is even a "buttery tomato sauce," in which basil makes its very first appearance.[149]

Dressing pasta or tomato sauce with olive oil became "normal" only in the second half of the XX century.

GARLIC AND ONION, PEASANT AROMAS

B oth original to central Asia, garlic and onion have been cultivated for millennia and have invaded the world with their acrid and sweet aroma. Ancient medicine recognized their beneficial effect on the organism—also confirmed by contemporary modern science—and this image also accompanied the systematic use of these products as food.

They are often surrounded by a presumption of "vulgarity": in the Medieval literature, to smell of garlic and onion is a sign of peasant identity,[150] reinforced by the simplicity and ease of their procurement. The "theriac of peasants" was what garlic was called in dietetic texts, or rather a medicine for all sorts of maladies—but specifically for peasants, not for those who could afford the complicated concoction of vegetable and animal extracts that resulted in the precious *theriac*. But, as always, taste got the better of all intellectual prejudices, and cookbooks of all epochs reveal a widespread use of these products even in haute cuisine.[151]

Nevertheless, with regard to our story, garlic and onion come on the scene rather late. As long as pasta was dressed with butter and cheese, perhaps with the addition of "sweet spices" such as cinnamon or sugar, there was no felt need for garlic or onion, and no cookbook recommended their use. It was not until the advent of tomato sauce—that is, for spaghetti, the XIX century—that these two ancient kitchen and table companions were welcomed as part of the recipe.

At this point, which one to choose? Everyone will have their favorite, but let's give the floor to Pellegrino Artusi who has no doubts in wanting both of them to flavor his sauce: "prepare a battuto with a quarter of an onion, a clove of garlic" and so on.[152]

A Touch of Green

A rtusi's recipe also calls for "a few basil leaves," which accompany the garlic and onion, and a bit of celery and parsley. Over time, basil has become an inevitable ingredient of our dish, an *identifying* element, to the point of acquiring in the iconography of the media an immediately understandable symbolic value. The green of the basil, together with the red of the tomato sauce and the white of the spaghetti (or in some cases of mozzarella) is by now an easy device for evoking the Italian flag.

But even this ultimate touch of green does not appear to be particularly old. Basil, native to India and perhaps also to tropical Africa, was cultivated in the Mediterranean starting in classical times, but only occasionally and only as a medicinal plant. Its use in cooking came late, not least because of the less than encouraging judgments it received in dietetic texts. Galen believed it was harmful to the stomach, heavy to digest, and a generator of bad humors.[153]

Its bad reputation continued into the Middle Ages and, as late as the XV century, the humanist Bartolomeo Platina, citing the testimony of the physician Chrysippus, reported in Pliny's *Natural History*, accuses basil of damaging the stomach, weakening eyesight, corroding the liver, and even causing madness. That is why, he says, goats refuse to eat this plant. Some even claimed that scorpions could be born from basil if it was crushed and covered with a rock; or worms and lice if it was chewed and exposed to the sun. Platina admitted, however, that all these things "are denied by experience" and thus allows us to understand that basil was indeed used, even though his advice was to use it with parsimony, given "the excessive power that comes [to this herb] from its hot and dry nature."[154]

Platina's considerations reveal a certain change in the way of representing the properties of basil, but medieval cookbooks continued to prefer other aromatic herbs. In Italy, basil was decidedly less popular than thyme, marjoram, and mint. Not until the 1500s do we see explicit attestations of a culinary use of basil. Around 1565-70, the botanist and gastronome Costanzo Felici defines it as "much used in salads and in soups and in many other dishes, making use of its leaves and tender tops," so that "in summer there are no gardens or windows that are not adorned with it and there is no plant that women plant more willingly than this one."[155] *Women*; as in numerous other cases, it is to them that Felici attributes the merit for a gastronomic innovation that would soon become a tradition. In the next century, Giacomo Castelvetro would also ascribe to the *massare* (housewives) the capacity to make salads of "good herbs," shrewdly selecting "a certain proportion of parsley, chard, mint, basil, and thyme," to then make it into a "mischianza" (mix) suitable for dressing "many foods."[156]

We can conclude that basil's entrance into Italian cooking does not date back to before the XVI-XVII centuries.

To find it in tomato sauce—and hence potentially on spaghetti—we will have to wait until 1837, the year of publication of Ippolito Cavalcanti's *Cucina teorico-pratica*, the cookbook of Neapolitan haute cuisine supplemented two years later by an appendix on popular cooking.[157] Then, as usual, it will be up to Artusi. But a lot of water would go over the dam before basil became a symbol of Italian gastronomy.

THE SPAGHETTI TREE

On April 1, 1957, the BBC broadcast a documentary on Italian cooking, showing spaghetti trees, which had produced a magnificent harvest that year.[158] The television show recalled the spaghetti plantations in the Po valley, the lucky disappearance of the "spaghetti worm," the skill of the Italian agronomists who had developed new varieties of spaghetti, the standardized length that allowed for speedier mechanized picking. A return to the mythical Land of Cockaigne? Actually, a practical joke (it *was* April Fool's Day), but some viewers may have taken it seriously. "In 1950s Great Britain," David Gentilcore has observed, "this dish was still mysterious and exotic," albeit already a synonym for Italian cooking.

But spaghetti with tomato sauce would risk being an unknown dish even to Italians, if we were to think of it as a simple object, present "since forever" on our dinner tables, *original* to our culture and the fruit of *our* roots, which "naturally" attest to its being a constitutive element of Italian identity. Thinking of it in this way would amount to stepping outside of history and into legend, ignoring the complexity of the itineraries that have marked the evolution of this dish, through successive stratifications that have brought into play a variety of peoples and cultures, and changing experiences and tastes. I hope that the pages of this book have managed to illustrate that clearly.

The history of our plate of spaghetti, the search for its origins and its roots—economic, social, political, cultural—has forced us to travel to multiple lands and to come to terms with eating habits, ways of production, and culinary procedures distant from each other in time and space. A long series of innovations, developed in different times and places, have contributed to creating this tradition so typically Italian.

During our journey, we have encountered ancient, medieval, and modern products; ancient and medieval products revisited in modern usage; modern products used in conformity with ancient customs; products abandoned along the way while others replaced them; combinations at times predictable and at times surprising.

This little big history has shown us—in the concreteness of a plate of spaghetti—that *identity* does not correspond to *roots*. Our identity is what we are. Our roots are *not* "what we were" but rather the encounters, exchanges, and crossings that have transformed what we were into what we are. And the deeper we go in search of our origins, the more our roots extend and grow away from us—just as it happens with plants. To follow the metaphor all the way down, we discover that our roots, quite often, are *others*. Searching for the origins of what we are may just be, therefore, a way of getting to know others. The others who live in us.

Notes

Words: Handle with Care

[1] M. Bloch, *The Historian's Craft,* New York, Alfred A. Knopf, 1953.

[2] M. Bettini, *Contro le radici*, Bologna, il Mulino, 2012 (essay edited and expanded in *Radici. Tradizione, identità, memoria*, Bologna, il Mulino, 2016).

[3] F. Remotti, *Contro l'identità*, Roma-Bari, Laterza, 2007.

Recipes and Products, Or Rather, Time and Space

[4] O. Lando, *Commentario delle più notabili et mostruose cose d'Italia et altri luoghi [. . .] con un breve catalogo de gli inventori delle cose che si mangiano et beveno*, G. e P. Salvatori (ed.), Bologna, Pendragon, 1994 (taken from the Venetian edition of 1553; the first edition is dated 1548).

[5] A. Capatti, M. Montanari, *La cucina italiana. Storia di una cultura*, Roma-Bari, Laterza, 1999, p. 14.

Reflecting on a Plate of Pasta

[6] M. Montanari, *L'identità italiana in cucina*, Roma-Bari, Laterza, 2010.

[7] O. Redon, B. Laurioux, "La constitution d'une nouvelle catégorie culinaire? Les pâtes dans les livres de cuisine italiens de la fin du Moyen Age," *Médiévales*, 16-17 (1989), pp. 51-60, at p. 51.

Marco Polo and Spaghetti: The Birth of a Fake News Item

[8] "Contre Marco Polo: une histoire comparée des pâtes alimentaires," *Médiévales*, 16-17 (1989), pp. 25-100.

[9] On this question, see G. Blue, "Marco Polo et les pâtes," *Médiévales*, 20 (1991), pp. 91-98.

[10] *The Macaroni Journal*, October 1929, pp. 32-34.

[11] S. Serventi, F. Sabban, *La pasta. Storia e cultura di un cibo universale*, Roma-Bari, Laterza, 2000, pp. 345 et seq.

BREAD AND PASTA: FROM THE MIDDLE EAST TO EUROPE

[12] M. Oubahli, *La main et le pétrin. Alimentation céréalière et pratiques culinaires en Occident musulman au Moyen Âge*, Casablanca, Fondation du Roi Abdul-Aziz Al Saoud pour les Études Islamiques et les Sciences Humaines, 2012, pp. 397-398.

[13] Ibid. p. 388.

[14] J. Bottéro, *Textes culinaires mésopotamiens*, Winona Lake, Eisenbrauns, 1995, p. 33.

[15] J. André, *L'alimentation et la cuisine à Rome*, Paris, Les Belles Lettres, 1981, p. 211; Oubahli, *La main* cit., p. 390.

[16] B. Laurioux, *Des lasagnes romaines aux vermicelles arabes: quelques réflexions sur les pâtes alimentaires*, in Id., *Une histoire culinaire du Moyen Âge*, Paris, Champion, 2005, pp. 213-230, at p. 219.

[17] Apicius, *De re coquinaria*, V, 1, 3 (ed. J. André, *L'art culinaire*, Paris, Les Belles Lettres, 1974).

[18] Serventi-Sabban, *La pasta* cit., pp. 16-19.

[19] L. Sada, V. Valente, *Liber de coquina*, Bari, Puglia Grafica Sud, 1995, p. 150 (III, 9).

[20] So it is in the cookbook attributed to Apicius, where the *tracta* is cooked in milk and water (*De arte coquinaria* cit., loc. cit.: "Tres orbiculos tractae siccas et confringis et partibus in lac summittis. Ne uratur, aquam miscendo agitabis").

[21] Serventi-Sabban, *La pasta* cit., pp. 28-29.

NEW NAMES FOR A NEW PRODUCT

[22] See above, p. 20 (and note 17).

[23] Laurioux, *Des lasagnes* cit., p. 226.

[24] Oubahli, *La main* cit., pp. 366, 389.

[25] Ibid, p. 368.

[26] Ibid. pp. 344-347. The generic meaning of *itriyya* will also remain in the West but only in dietetic texts, while cookbooks will tend to give it a specific meaning of long, thin pasta.

[27] Ibid, p. 385.

The Sicilian Melting Pot and the Birth of the Pasta Industry

[28] Idrisi, *Il libro di Ruggero*, U. Rizzitano, Palermo, Flaccovio (ed.) (1966), p. 38.

[29] On the contrary, it is a Neapolitan gentleman who, to insult a Sicilian, uses the epithet 'manciamaccheroni' (macaronieater), in a play from 1569 (*La vedova* di Giambattista Cini) cited by Emilio Sereni and before him by Benedetto Croce (cf. E. Sereni, *Note di storia dell'alimentazione nel Mezzogiorno: i Napoletani da "mangiafoglia" a mangiamaccheroni"*, in Id., *Terra nuova e buoi rossi*, Turin, Einaudi, 1981, pp. 292-371 [previously in *Cronache meridionali*, IV-V-VI (1958)], a p. 300). For the "transfer" of the nickname from Sicilians to Neapolitans see below pp. 47 et seq.

[30] For what follows, see Serventi-Sabban, *La pasta* cit., pp. 59 et seq.

[31] L. Galoppini, "Le commerce des pâtes alimentaires dans les Aduanas Sardas," *Médiévales*, 36 (1999), pp. 111-127.

[32] Serventi-Sabban, *La pasta* cit., p. 47.

[33] Oubahli, *La main* cit., p. 387.

[34] M. Montanari, *Il cibo come cultura*, Roma-Bari, Laterza, 2004, pp. 19-22; Id., *Gusti del Medioevo. I prodotti, la cucina, la tavola*, Roma-Bari, Laterza, 2012, pp. 190-191.

When Spaghetti Were Called Macaroni

[35] Laurioux, *Des lasagnes* cit., p. 213.

[36] A. Martellotti, *I ricettari di Federico II. Dal "Meridionale" al "Liber de coquina,"* Florence, Olschki, 2005, has proposed a complex reconstruction of the cookbook, comparing it to other coeval cookbooks and tying them all to a lost cookbook from the Swabian era. The various texts are published and compared in an appendix.

[37] Sada-Valente, *Liber de coquina* cit., pp. 44-45, 176.

[38] Serventi-Sabban, *La pasta* cit., p. 34.

[39] Oubahli, *La main* cit., p. 482.

[40] Capatti-Montanari, *La cucina italiana* cit., pp. 67 et seq.

[41] C. Benporat, *Cucina italiana del Quattrocento*, Florence, Olschki, 1996, pp. 107, 183, 237.

[42] Ibid, pp. 105, 183, 237.

[43] A. Martellotti, *Linguistica e cucina*, Florence, Olschki, 2012, p. 148. The word appears as a nickname in documents in the area of Salerno, site of the famous medical school (at 1041: *Mackarone*), and in Sicily (at 1156: *Maccarrone*). Areas, Martellotti observes, with a strong Islamic influence. Hence the suggestion that the word derives

from the Arabic *muqarrada* (= dough made from sugar and pistachios and almonds, cut into portions), whose meaning shifted out of the pastry field in Italian while remaining in that field in French and English, where *macaron* is still today a sweet of that kind. Other etymologies have been proposed for "maccherone," the least probable being the one that links it to the verb *maccare = ammaccare*, make dough (ibid., p. 147).

[44] Benporat, *Cucina italiana* cit., p. 184. In the same way, "vermicelli," when done put them out in the sun to dry and they too "will last two or three years" (ibid.).

[45] Ibid., pp. 183-184. Among the various manuscripts of Maestro Martino's cookbook, all collected in the Bemporad volume, only the one in the historical archive of Riva di Garda includes Genoese macaroni.

[46] S. Battaglia, *Grande dizionario della lingua italiana*, under *spaghetti*.

[47] Ibid. under *maccherone*: "Long pasta, but in different shapes depending on the region (spaghetti, bucatini, fusilli, etc.)" By extension "every type of pasta that is eaten dried."

A New Category of Food

[48] So says Oubahli, *La main* cit., p. 343, contesting the opposing opinion of B. Rosenberger, "Les pâtes dans le monde musulman," *Médiévales*, 16-17 (1989), pp. 77-98, at p. 79.

[49] F. Sabban, *Ravioli cristallins et tagliatelles rouges: les pâtes chinoises entre XIIe et XIVe siècle*, pp. 29-50.

[50] Redon-Laurioux, *La constitution* op cit.

[51] Sereni, *Note di storia dell'alimentazione* op cit., p. 327; M. Nicoud, *L'adaptation du discours diététique aux pratiques alimentaires: l'exemple de Barnabas de Reggio*, "Mélanges de l'École Française de Rome, Moyen Âge," 107, 1995, 1, pp. 207-231, at p. 217. Serventi-Sabban, *La pasta* op cit., p. 25, notes that the vernacular use of *tria* in the Ancona area "testifies to its Greek rather than Arab origin, given that the region remained under Greek influence throughout the early Middle Ages, far out of the range of Arab civilization." This takes nothing away from what we have said about the role that, in any case, Arab culture played in the spread of the term (and of its new meaning) in the West. The name *tria* still survives in the dialects of southern Italy, for example, in the recipes for "ciceri and tria" widely known in Puglia (Martellotti, *Linguistica* op cit., p. 140), while Ligurian "trenette" are said to have the same etymology.

[52] B. Reguardati, *Libellus de conservatione sanitatis*, composed

between 1435 and 1438 and published for the first time in Rome by Filippo de Lignamine in 1475. Cf. Laurioux, *Des lasagnes* op cit., p. 215.

[53] *Tractado utilissimo circa la conservatione de la sanidade*, Milan, Pietro de Corneno, 1481.

[54] M. Savonarola, *Libreto de tutte le cosse che se magnano. Un'opera di dietetica del sec. XV*, J. Nystedt (ed.), Stockholm, Almqvist & Wiskell, 1988, p. 62.

[55] Laurioux, *Des lasagnes* op cit., p. 202.

[56] C. Felici, *Scritti naturalistici*, I, *Del'insalata e piante che in qualunque modo vengono per cibo del'homo*, G. Arbizzoni (ed.) Urbino, Quattro Venti, 1986, p. 117.

HOW DO YOU COOK PASTA?

[57] Montanari, *Il cibo come cultura* op cit., pp. 63 et seq.

[58] Uguccione da Pisa, *Derivationes*, Enzo Cecchini (ed.), Firenze, SISMEL-Edizioni del Galluzzo, 2004, L 10.4, p. 642: "*laganum, quoddam genus cibi quod prius in aqua coquitur, postea in oleo frigitur.*" Lasagna, Uguccione observes, can also be fried directly in oil but only when they are destined to become sweets with honey: "*sunt lagana de pasta quasi quedam membranule, que quandoque statim in oleo friguntur postea melle condiuntur.*" In this case their name changes to *crustella*. True *lasania*, even if fried, "*prius in aqua coquuntur.*" According to A.F. Buccini, *Lasagna: A Layered History*, in *Wrapped & Stuffed Foods: Proceedings of the Oxford Symposium on Food and Cookery 2012*, M. McWilliams (ed.), Devon, Prospect Books, 2013, pp. 94-104, at p. 96, this is the oldest medieval description of *laganae*.

[59] Benporat, *Cucina italiana* op cit., pp. 107-108.

[60] Laurioux, *Des lasagnes* op cit., p. 224; Oubahli, *La main* op cit., p. 470.

CHEESE ON MACARONI

[61] Another ideal pairing was cheese and pears. Cf. M. Montanari, *Il formaggio con le pere. La storia in un proverbio*, Rome-Bari, Laterza, 2008.

[62] Reguardati, *Libellus de conservatione sanitatis* op cit., cap. XXXI-III, *de caseo*: "*Ad talium viscosorum humorum generationum aptissimus est caseus et proprie cum macharonibus, laganiis et ferculis de pasta comestus . . .*"

[63] Sada-Valente, *Liber de coquina* op cit., III, 9, p. 150.

[64] Montanari, *Gusti del Medioevo* op cit., p. 98.

[65] B. Platina, *De honesta voluptate et valetudine. Un trattato sui piaceri della tavola e la buona salute*, new edition with commentary by E. Carnevale Schianca (ed.), Florence, Olschki, 2015, p. 157.

[66] I. Naso, *Formaggi del Medioevo La "Summa lacticiniorum,"* Pantaleone da Confienza, Turin, Il Segnalibro, 1990, pp. 114-116.

[67] Montanari, *Il formaggio con le pere* op cit., pp. 31-38.

[68] Braudel, "Alimentation et catégories de l'histoire," in J.J. Hémardinquer (ed.), *Pour une histoire de l'alimentation*, Paris, Armand Colin, 1970 (Cahiers des Annales, 28), pp. 15-19, at p. 17: "Les aliments entre eux, les boissons entre elles, tous, liquides et solides, se querellent, s'opposent, s'ajoutent, se substituent les uns aux autres. Que ne parlons-nous, à l'image des nos collègues géographes ou botanistes, d'associations alimentaires, comme ils parlent d'associations végétales!" The brief and dense essay by Braudel, presented in this volume as a methodological introduction, had appeared in *Annales ESC*, 16 (1961), pp. 723-728, to open the French review's investigation of dietary regimens.

[69] L. Messedaglia, "Leggendo la Cronica di frate Salimbene da Parma. Note per la storia della vita economica e del costume nel secolo XIII," *Atti dell'Istituto veneto di scienze, lettere ed arti*, CIII (1943-44), part II, pp. 351-426, at p. 385; Sereni, *Note di storia dell'alimentazione*, op cit., p. 326.

[70] P. Aretino, *Sei giornate* [1534-36], G. Aquilecchia (ed.) Bari, Laterza, 1969, p. 127.

[71] G. Boccaccio, *Decameron*, Day VIII, novella 3.

[72] G. Mori, A. Perin (ed.), *Il mito del paese di Cuccagna. Immagini a stampa dalla Raccolta Bertarelli*, Pisa, ETS, 2015, pp. 64-70.

[73] The "ravioli" that Boccaccio had in mind were different; in all probability he was alluding to meatballs that could be, when called for, wrapped in a piece of pasta wound around itself to form a sort of small cake: a *tortello* which wraps around the raviolo. The two terms are often distinct in the medieval and Renaissance lexicon (cf. Capatti-Montanari, *La cucina italiana* op cit., pp. 72-74) before becoming confused in modern use. But in this case, too, the preferred association with cheese does not change.

ANOTHER WAY TO EAT: THE FORK

[74] Montanari, *Gusti del Medioevo* op cit., pp. 238-244.

[75] See below, pp. 58, 71.

[76] Sada-Valente, *Liber de coquina* op cit., III, 64. Cf. Capatti-Montanari, *La cucina italiana* op cit., p. 61.

[77] F. Sacchetti, *Il Trecentonovelle*, CXXIV, A. Borlenghi (ed.), Milan, Rizzoli, 1957, pp. 387-390).

[78] M. Montanari, *Il sugo della storia*, Roma-Bari, Laterza, 2016, pp. 54-56.

PASTA CHANGES ITS STATUS

[79] See above, the chapter "The Sicilian Melting Pot and the Birth of the Pasta Industry."

[80] Sereni, *Note di storia dell'alimentazione* op cit., pp. 321-322.

[81] Serventi-Sabban, *La pasta* op cit., pp. 100-112.

[82] C. Messisbugo, *Banchetti composizioni di vivande e apparecchio generale*, F. Bandini (ed.), Vicenza, Neri Pozza, 1992, p. 22 (orig. publ. Ferrara, Buglhat e Hucher, 1549). The book was republished some years later with another title: *Libro novo nel qual s'insegna a far d'ogni sorte di vivanda secondo la diversità dei tempi*, Venetia, al segno di San Girolamo, 1552.

[83] Serventi-Sabban, *La pasta* op cit., p. 111.

[84] Sereni, *Note di storia dell'alimentazione* op cit., p. 348, citing *Nuova canzonetta in diversi linguaggi*, an anonymous text from the end of the 1600s, published in Venice, which passes in review the conventional features attributed to the inhabitants of this or that city. At one point, a Neapolitan man makes his entrance and invites some people who are arguing "*a mangiar li macaroni*" (to eat macaroni). The complexity of the economic, social, and political factors that account for this change has been illustrated by A. De Bernardi, *Gli italiani a tavola. Storia sociale della pasta*, Roma, Donzelli, 2019.

[85] Sada-Valente, *Liber de coquina* op cit., II, 62, p. 144.

[86] B. Scappi, *Opera*, Venetia, Tramezzino, 1570, cc. 228, 241*v*, 291.

AL DENTE

[87] F. Parasecoli, *Al dente. A history of food in Italy*, Islington-London, Reaktion Books, 2014.

[88] Benporat, *Cucina italiana* op cit., pp. 107, 183, 237.

[89] Scappi, *Opera* op cit., II, CLXXIIII, c. 70*r*.

[90] G. Del Turco, *Epulario e segreti vari. Trattati di cucina toscana nella Firenze seicentesca*, A. Evangelista (ed.), Bologna, Forni, 1992, p. 28.

[91] A. Latini, *Lo scalco alla moderna*, I, Napoli, Parrino e Mutii, 1692, p. 301.

[92] Serventi-Sabban, *La pasta* op cit., p. 326. Serventi-Sabban, *La pasta* op cit., p. 326.

[93] I. Cavalcanti, *Cucina teorico-pratica col corrispondente riposto*, Naples, Palma, 1839, pp. 364-365.

[94] P. Artusi, *Science in the Kitchen and the Art of Eating Well*, Murtha Baca (transl.), Toronto, University of Toronto Press, 2003, recipe n. 85, p. 94.

WE ARE WHAT WE EAT

[95] F. La Cecla, *La pasta e la pizza*, Bologna, il Mulino, 1998, pp. 27-28. Ibid, p. 17, the letter of Cavour of July 26, 1860, written in French, which I have freely translated into Italian. For the letter of September 7, see G. Mantovano, *L'avventura del cibo*, Rome, Gremese, 1989, p. 83. Cf. Montanari, *L'identità italiana in cucina* op cit., p. 51.

[96] V. Teti, *Le culture alimentari nel Mezzogiorno continentale in età contemporanea*, in *Storia d'Italia. Annali*, 13, *L'alimentazione*, A. Capatti, A. De Bernardi, A. Varni, (eds.) Turin, Einaudi, 1998, pp. 63-165, at p. 97.

[97] Ibid., p. 98.

WHITE AND RED

[98] D. Gentilcore, *La purpurea meraviglia. Storia del pomodoro in Italia*, Milan, Garzanti, 2010, p. 101.

[99] Ibid., pp. 11-12, citing P.A. Mattioli, *Di Pedacio Dioscoride Anazarbeo libri cinque della historia et materia medicinale tradotti in lingua volgare*, Venetia, De Bascarini, 1544; Id., *Commentarii in libros sex Pedacii Dioscoridis Anazarbei, de medica materia*, Venetiis, Vincentium Valgrisium, 1554, p. 479.

[100] Ibid., pp. 11-12, citing P.A. Mattioli, *Di Pedacio Dioscoride Anazarbeo libri cinque della historia et materia medicina-le tradotti in lingua volgare*, Venetia, De Bascarini, 1544; Id., *Commentarii in libros sex Pedacii Dioscoridis Anazarbei, de medica materia*, Venetiis, Vincentium Valgrisium, 1554, p. 479.

[101] P.A. Michiel, *I cinque libri di piante* [1553-65], E. De Toni, Venezia, Carlo Ferrari (eds.), 1940, p. 227. Cf. Gentilcore, *La purpurea meraviglia* op cit., pp. 20-24.

[102] C. Durante, *Herbario Nuovo*, Roma, Bartholomeo Bonfadino and Tito Diani, 1585, p. 372.

[103] G.D. Sala, *De alimentis* [1628], in Ibid., *Ars medica*, Patavii,

Franciscus Bolzetta, 1641 (cited by Gentilcore, *La purpurea meraviglia* op cit., p. 28).

[104] Felici, *Del'insalata* op cit., pp. 89-90.

[105] Gentilcore, *La purpurea meraviglia* op cit., p. 30 (with reference to the late XVI century treatise by G. Soderini, *Della cultura degli orti e giardini*, Florence, Stamperia del Giglio, 1814).

[106] Ibid, p. 11.

SPANISH TOMATO SAUCE

[107] Ibid, p. 68.

[108] Latini, *Lo scalco alla moderna*, I, op cit., p. 444. Cf. II, 1694, p. 162.

[109] V. Corrado, *Del cibo pitagorico ovvero erbaceo*, Rome, Donzelli, 2001, p. 76.

[110] Ibid., *Il cuoco galante*, Naples, Stamperia Raimondiana, 1773, XIV, 1.

A FELICITOUS ENCOUNTER

[111] Gentilcore, *La purpurea meraviglia* op cit., p. 117.

[112] Corrado, *Del cibo pitagorico* op cit., p. 76.

[113] [M.F.], *La cucina casereccia*, L. Mancusi Sorrentino (ed.), Naples, Grimaldi, 1993, p. 31. The cookbook was reprinted several times in the following decades, enlarged from the second edition (1808) on by four treatises on fruit preserves, wines, ice cream, and rose liqueurs. The anonymous author signed the frontispiece of editions after the first. The edition used here is the seventh (1828).

[114] Ibid, p. 47.

[115] Ibid, *Introduction*, p. xxi.

[116] Ibid, pp. 55-56. On the history of the macaroni casserole (or pie), see Martellotti, *Linguistica e cucina* op cit., pp. 99-112.

[117] Montanari, *L'identità italiana in cucina* op cit., pp. 23-32, on the decisive importance of the popular culture/elite culture nexus in the construction of Italian gastronomic heritage.

[118] Cavalcanti, *Cucina teorico-pratica* op cit., p. 393.

[119] Ibid, p. 365.

[120] A. Spatuzzi, L. Somma, *Sull'alimentazione del popolo minuto in Napoli*, Naples, Stamperia della Regia Università, 1863 (cited by Gentilcore, *La purpurea meraviglia* op cit., p. 91).

[121] M. Montanari, *Le ragioni di un successo*, in G. Frosini, M. Montanari (ed.), *Il secolo artusiano*, Florence, Accademia della Crusca, 2012, pp. 7-15.

[122] Artusi, *Science in the Kitchen*, op cit., recipe n. 125 (pp. 120-121).

A SPICE FOR EVERYONE

[123] N. Monardes, *Delle cose che vengono portate dall'Indie Occidentali pertinenti l'uso della medicina*, Venice, Ziletti, 1582, part I, p. 39 (original in Spanish, 1569). Cf. M. Sentieri, G. Zazzu, *I semi dell'Eldorado. L'alimentazione in Europa dopo la scoperta dell'America*, Bari, Dedalo, 1992, p. 129.

[124] F. Braudel, *Civilization and Capitalism*, I, *The Structures of Everyday Life*, Berkeley, University of California Press, 1992, p. 222.

[125] M. Montanari, *La fame e l'abbondanza. Storia dell'alimentazione in Europa*, Rome-Bari, Laterza, 1993, pp. 145-150.

[126] G.F. de Oviedo, *Della naturale e generale istoria dell'Indie* (1535), in G.B. Ramusio, *Navigazioni e viaggi* [1556], Turin, Einaudi, V, 1985, pp. 590-591. Cf. V. Teti, *Storia del peperoncino. Un protagonista delle culture mediterranee*, Rome, Donzelli, 2007, p. 42.

[127] Monardes, *Delle cose che vengono portate dall'Indie Occidentali* op cit., pp. 38-39.

[128] P.A. Mattioli, *Discorsi nelli sei libri di Pedacio Dioscoride Anazarbeo della materia medicinale, hora di nuovo dal suo stesso autore ricorretti e in mille luoghi aumentati*, Venice, Valgrisi, 1568, p. 608. Cited in Sentieri-Zazzu, *I semi dell'Eldorado* op cit., p. 128.

[129] See above, p. 63 (and note 107).

[130] See above, p. 64 (and note 108).

[132] V. Agnoletti, *La nuova cucina economica*, Rome, Poggioli, 1819, II, p. 189. The first edition is from 1803. I'm citing here from A. Capatti, note (at p. 186) to the Italian edition of Artusi, *La scienza in cucina* op cit.

OLIVE OIL AND THE INVENTION OF THE MEDITERRANEAN DIET

[133] E. Moro, *La dieta mediterranea. Mito e storia di uno stile di vita*, Bologna, il Mulino, 2014.

[134] N.K. Sandars (ed.), *L'epopea di Gilgameš*, Milan, Adelphi, 1986, p. 92 (where, due to an error in translation, it speaks of wine and not beer)

[135] André, *L'alimentation et la cuisine à Rome* op cit., pp. 181-185.

[136] Montanari, *La fame e l'abbondanza* op cit., pp. 20-21.

[137] Ibid., *Mangiare da cristiani*, Milano, Rizzoli, 2015, pp. 107 et seq.

[138] J.-L. Flandrin, *Il gusto e la necessità*, Milan, Il Saggiatore, 1994 (orig. ed., "Le goût et la nécéssité: sur l'usage des graisses dans les

cuisines d'Europe occidentale," *Annales ESC*, XXXVIII, 1983, pp. 369-401).

[139] Montanari, *Gusti del Medioevo* op cit., p. 106.

[140] Ibid, p. 107. For an example of equivalence between oil and butter as fats usable on days of abstinence, cf. the *Cooking Register* of Johannes Bockenheim, chef for Pope Martin V in the 1430s. In the part of the *registrum* devoted to the Lenten period, there is an indication to dress bean soup "*cum oleo olive, vel butiro*"; for carp casserole, to cook them with wine, parsley, "*oleo, vel butiro*" (B. Laurioux, "Le 'Registre de cuisine' de Giovanni Bockenheym, cuisinier du pape Martin V," *Mélanges de l'École Française de Rome*, 100, 1988, pp. 709-760, n. 61, p. 740; n. 63, pp. 740-741).

[141] Benporat, *Cucina italiana* op cit., pp. 107, 183.

[142] Lando, *Commentario* op cit., p. 9.

[143] C. Malespini, *Novelle*, E. Allodoli, Lanciano, Carabba (eds.), 1915, Nov. VII, p. 64.

[144] Mori-Perin, *Il mito del paese di Cuccagna* op cit., loc. cit.

[145] Felici, *Del'insalata* op cit., p. 117: pasta can be dressed "with oil or with walnuts or with almonds or with milk or with cheese or with peppers and other spices."

[146] Latini, *Lo scalco alla moderna*, I, op cit., p. 444. See above, p. 64 (and note 108).

[147] Cavalcanti, *Cucina teorico-pratica* cit., p. 393. See above, p. 69 (and note 118).

[148] Ibid, p. 365.

[149] Ibid, p. 181.

GARLIC AND ONION, PEASANT AROMAS

[150] M. Montanari, *L'alimentazione contadina nell'alto Medioevo*, Naples, Liguori, 1979, p. 467.

[151] Ibid., *Gusti del Medioevo* op cit., p. 186.

[152] Artusi, *Science in the Kitchen* cit., recipe n. 125 (ed. op cit., p. 121).

A TOUCH OF GREEN

[153] C. Galeno, *De alimentorum facultatibus libri tres*, Paris, Colinaeum, c. 1530, 69v (cited by E. Carnevale Schianca, *La cucina medievale. Lessico, storia, preparazioni*, Florence, Olschki, 2011, p. 66).

[154] Platina, *De honesta voluptate* op cit., III, 29 (ed. op cit., p. 194). The account of the physician Chrysippus of Cnidos in Pliny the Elder, *Natural History*, XX, pp. 119-120.

[155] Felici, *Del'insalata* op cit., pp. 66-67.

[156] G. Castelvetro, *Brieve racconto di tutte le radici di tutte l'erbe e di tutti i frutti che crudi o cotti in Italia si mangiano*, E. Faccioli (ed.), Mantua, Arcari, 1988, p. 15.

[157] Cavalcanti, *Cucina teorico-pratica* op cit., p. 181.

THE SPAGHETTI TREE

[158] Gentilcore, *La purpurea meraviglia* op cit., p. 226.

Index of Names